英诗汉韵——译诗如诗探步

English Poems in Chinese Poetic Forms
Or as Attempted

英诗汉韵

译诗如诗探步

English Poems in Chinese Poetic Forms
Or as Attempted

陶志健 译

Acer Books

英诗汉韵——译诗如诗探步（红枫丛书之八）
汉译：陶志健
封面摄影：陶志健
出版：Acer Books

书号：978-1-7381938-6-8

红枫丛书
策划：黎杨
设计：陶志健

English Poems in Chinese Poetic Forms
Chinese Translator: Tao, Zhijian
Publisher: Acer Books
Cover Photo: Tao, Zhijian

ISBN: 978-1-7381938-6-8

Copyright © 2024 Tao Zhijian.

All rights reserved. No part of this book, except contents in the public domain, may be reproduced or used in any manner without the prior written permission of the copyright owner, except for the use of brief quotations in critical articles and book reviews.
E-mail: acerbookscanada@gmail.com

目 录

目 录 1
译诗如诗探步 5
菲利普・西德尼 1
   阿斯托菲和斯黛拉之 31 1
   Astrophil and Stella - Sonnet 31 3
威廉・莎士比亚 4
   商籁体之十八 4
   Sonnet 18 5
   商籁体之六十六 6
   Sonnet 66 8
   "活着，还是不活" 9
   "To Be or Not to Be" 11
约翰・邓恩 13
   神圣商赖体之十 13
   Holy Sonnet X 15
安德鲁・马维尔 16
   致他的忸怩女友 16
   To His Coy Mistress 19
亚历山大・蒲伯 21
   独居赋 21

目录

Ode on Solitude 24

奥利弗·哥尔德史密斯 25

   当可爱的女人失足犯傻 25

   When Lovely Woman Stoops to Folly 26

安娜·拉埃蒂茨娅·巴鲍德 27

   生命若何我不知 27

   Life! I Know Not What Thou Art 29

威廉·布莱克 31

   啊！向阳花 31

   Ah! Sun-flower 32

   永恒 33

   Eternity 34

威廉·华兹华斯 35

   草的辉煌 35

   Splendour in the Grass 36

   独荡似闲云 37

   我独自游荡像一片闲云 38

   I Wandered Lonely as a Cloud 40

   作于西敏寺桥上 41

   Composed upon Westminster Bridge 43

沃尔特·萨维奇·兰德 53

   一世无争 53

   I Strove with None 54

拉尔夫·沃尔多·爱默生 44

   紫杜鹃 44

   The Rhodora 45

目录

艾米莉·狄金森 46
 未能停步等死神 46
 Because I could not stop for Death 47
威廉·巴特勒·叶芝 49
 二次降临 49
 The Second Coming 51
 智慧随着时光而来 52
 The Coming Of Wisdom With Time 52
埃兹拉·庞德 53
 致意 55
 Salutation 56
托马斯·斯特恩斯·艾略特 57
 荒　原 57
 The Waste Land 93
 J.阿尔弗雷德·普鲁弗洛克的情歌 117
 The Love Song of J. Alfred Prufrock 126
切斯瓦夫·米沃什 133
 福赐 133
 Gift 135
狄兰·托马斯 136
 而死亡也不能主宰 136
 And Death Shall Have no Dominion 138
 不要驯然遁入那个长夜 140
 Do not go gentle into that good night 142
莱昂纳德·科恩 143
 一千个吻之深 143

目录

A Thousand Kisses Deep 146
凯伦·索利 148
 人生就是一场狂欢 148
 Life is a Carnival 150
 北方 152
 The North 154
 改建 155
 Conversion 157

译诗如诗探步

自序

所谓"英诗"者，然也；"汉韵"者，以不同的方式趋然，也即尽力使然也。

这个集子，也可算是个大杂烩：从 16 世纪的西德尼，到 21 世纪的索利；从格律严谨的维拉内尔（villanelle）和商籁体，到几无格律的当代诗；从虔诚的宗教情绪到玩世不恭的无奈；从苦恋悲情到及时行乐；从怡然享受生活到愤怒诅咒死亡；从深邃哲思若有所得到纯然感性无所适从；从厚重巨作到清雅小令；从英国到美国到加拿大，等等。可谓五花八门。但有一点却是有一致性的，他们所含以韵律为主体的诗歌风格得到重视和探究，并由译者在译文中尽己所能给予充分的大约等值的转达，也就是探究如何将原作的风格在最大程度上平移到译文中来。

窃以为，一首诗所用的韵律（或无韵律），无论是诗人自觉或不自觉的创作，也无论其与文字内容相关的紧密程度如何，都是诗人诗情的一种表达，都是他的诗作不可分割、不可忽略的成分，所以在这种意义上也都是一种内容，在翻译中都应该至少在一定程度上认作是"信"的范畴。在这个意义上，诗歌翻译的"信、达、雅"三个方面都不能脱离韵律形式而取得圆满。

说到"风格的平移"，实在是宽泛而言。何为"风格"，何为"平移"，何为"译诗如诗"，很难做严谨的界定。每一位意图做这种尝试的译家大概都有自己的认知和考量，见仁见智，各有所循。作为其中之一，笔者在这本书里所做的

 自序

努力，其自身也没有尊崇单一的模式，而是信马由缰，凭感觉而为。先前我曾表达过自己翻译诗歌的一点起因和考虑，也适用于此，略作调整，转抄如下：

众多经典英文诗歌，早有前辈筚路蓝缕，译介海内。时人译家亦众，各有千秋。然诗无达诂，自无达译。我因读诗，时觉译文略失忠信，偶欲献上所见；又常喜原作格律甚整，实为其诗不可或缺之品性要素，有望探寻如何以中文再现其妙。遂边玩边译，后又不断修改，终得本文所列之译本。然英文与中文差别甚巨，诗的格律更难相匹，确乃实情。故译文虽以中诗音韵节奏为基本，却未受严格的音韵限制，更无固定的对应格式；惟尽己所能，持守原诗意味，并体现其音韵节奏之感。未敢妄言兼顾，但求二者相衡。

应当说明，拙译尽管注重并探讨格律的表达和再现，却绝没有以其为重译所选诗歌之主要动因，也不敢以音韵而有损诗意内涵。重要的还是出于对原作理解的考量。如哈姆雷特的独白"活着还是不活"的译文，即是如此（见译文所附译者按）。我相信，原文用韵与否、如何用韵都只是手段，而达意传神才是目的；那么，译文也应该充分关注到这些手段并尽量采用相似或相近的手段，以便达到同样的达意传神的目的。

我要感谢 Karen Solie 授权翻译她的作品。另，诺奖诗人 Louise Glück 近逝，其作品的中文翻译权一时难以取得，遗憾拙译几首诗作暂未能排列书中。

是为序。

2024 年初春，蒙特利尔

菲利普·西德尼
Philip Sidney (1554–1586)

阿斯托菲和斯黛拉之 31

（商籁体）

举步何其忧伤，月啊，你爬向天空！
你是那样沉默，面容又那样苍白！
怎么，难道说即使于天堂的所在，
那闲不住的箭童也要舞弄利弓！
定然，如果你那见惯情爱的眼睛
善辨风情，当会体验苦恋的悲哀，
我从你脸上读出；你憔悴的容态
对同病相怜的我，道出你的苦情。
那么，同为情苦，月啊，请你相告：
一往情深在天上可算有欠聪敏？
那里的美人可如此间一样冷傲？
她们是否乐于博取别人的爱心，
却又将那些为情所困之人鄙弃？
她们视作美德的可是薄情寡义？

菲利普·西德尼 Philip Sidney

（五言体）

沉沉明月步，郁郁向天空。
默默君无语，苍苍尔面容。
缘何得若此，未解彼天宫：
莫道箭童劣，频频试射弓？
惯见花前事，君眸自慧明，
倘君真善辨，应感恋痴情，
观色吾知晓，相怜我共鸣，
憔憔君面貌，难掩尔私情。
同病相怜意，乞君相告明，
天宫轻笃恋，谓彼欠机灵？
上界如人世，佳人傲若冰？
碧霄仙女意，或爱戏痴情，
却把痴心汉，弃之随意凭？
美人评美品，寡义并薄情？

【译者记】这首诗是西德尼《阿斯托菲和斯黛拉（爱星者和星）》108 首商籁体系列中第 31 首，采用彼特拉克十四行诗格式：五部抑扬格，ABBA ABBA CDCDEE 韵法。拙译"商籁体"遵原韵法，"五言体"则仿五律格式。

菲利普·西德尼 Philip Sidney

Astrophil and Stella - Sonnet 31

With how sad steps, O Moon, thou climb'st the skies!
How silently, and with how wan a face!
What, may it be that even in heav'nly place
That busy archer his sharp arrows tries!
Sure, if that long-with-love-acquainted eyes
Can judge of love, thou feel'st a lover's case,
I read it in thy looks; thy languish'd grace
To me, that feel the like, thy state descries.
Then, ev'n of fellowship, O Moon, tell me,
Is constant love deem'd there but want of wit?
Are beauties there as proud as here they be?
Do they above love to be lov'd, and yet
Those lovers scorn whom that love doth possess?
Do they call virtue there ungratefulness?

威廉·莎士比亚
William Shakespeare (1564–1616)

商籁体之十八

我欲将君比夏日，
君比夏日更娇婉。
柔花五月遭风笞，
夏日匆匆期苦短。
天眼时时凭自烈，
黄金颜面亦常阴；
芳容芳色有时谢，
天灭天生无定因；
君之夏日永不涸，
君之美貌永不凋，
死神徒叹奈君何，
诗篇恒久君寿高。
人但呼吸眼但亮，
君随此作永流芳。

【译者记】莎翁此商籁体为三首四行诗加一个对句，五部抑扬格，ABAB CDCD EFEF GG 韵法。拙译采用中国诗词的七言句型，循原作之韵式而就，或可视作一种融合体。

威廉·莎士比亚 William Shakespeare

Sonnet 18

Shall I compare thee to a summer's day?
Thou art more lovely and more temperate.
Rough winds do shake the darling buds of May,
And summer's lease hath all too short a date.
Sometime too hot the eye of heaven shines,
And often is his gold complexion dimmed;
And every fair from fair sometime declines,
By chance, or nature's changing course, untrimmed;
But thy eternal summer shall not fade,
Nor lose possession of that fair thou ow'st,
Nor shall death brag thou wand'rest in his shade,
When in eternal lines to Time thou grow'st.
  So long as men can breathe, or eyes can see,
  So long lives this, and this gives life to thee.

威廉·莎士比亚 William Shakespeare

商籁体之六十六

（商籁体）

倦看这一切，惟愿安息，
见应有所养沦为乞丐，
那泼皮混混裹着锦衣，
那至纯之诚惨遭出卖，
那镀金荣耀耻置错处，
那良家贞女逼成娼妓，
那谦谦君子屈受羞辱，
那活力却被腐朽压抑，
那艺文横遭当局嗾斥，
那愚钝操刀挟制技能，
那简单真理被斥无知，
那良善被俘侍奉恶行。
　　厌倦这一切，亟欲远离，
　　此去惟不舍，吾爱孤凄。

威廉·莎士比亚 William Shakespeare

（排律）

厌倦世间诸等事，
但求一死长安息。
方闻应养生为丐，
又见泼皮裹锦衣；
忠信可悲遭背叛，
荣光无耻被挪移；
贞洁遭践成娼妓，
良善蒙羞官佬欺；
生力横遭衰朽废，
当局霸道艺文息；
痴愚持杖挟能巧，
明理无端被斥疑。
倦看世情思远去，
惟怜吾爱守孤凄。

【译者记】译文"排律"为求中文行文的平衡，将第一行译作两行，而将第七及第十四行合而为第八行。

另，虽同为莎翁商籁体，并同以七言体移译，第十八首用了原韵式，而这首却近乎排律。至于何者较为可取，尚待众家品鉴。

威廉·莎士比亚 William Shakespeare

Sonnet 66

Tir'd with all these, for restful death I cry,
As, to behold desert a beggar born,
And needy nothing trimm'd in jollity,
And purest faith unhappily forsworn,
And gilded honour shamefully misplac'd,
And maiden virtue rudely strumpeted,
And right perfection wrongfully disgrac'd,
And strength by limping sway disabled,
And art made tongue-tied by authority,
And folly—doctor-like—controlling skill,
And simple truth miscall'd simplicity,
And captive good attending captain ill.
   Tir'd with all these, from these would I be gone,
   Save that, to die, I leave my love alone.

威廉·莎士比亚 William Shakespeare

"活着,还是不活"
(哈姆雷特独白)

活着,还是不活:就是这个问题:
怎样才更为高贵:是逆来顺受
狂暴残忍之命运的飞石利箭,
还是拿起刀剑反抗无边的苦难,
豁出去结束一切?死了,睡了——
就完了,要是凭着安睡就能了结
心痛和那血肉之躯必然遭受的
千种折磨,这正是求之不得的
圆满结局啊。死了,睡了——
睡了,或许会作梦——唉,症结就在这儿,
因为当我们脱掉这苟活的皮囊,
在死亡的睡眠中会有怎样的梦,
定会让人裹足不前;就是这一条
它把漫漫一生酿成了灾难:
是啊,谁愿忍受时运的鞭挞和嘲弄、
暴君的欺凌、自大狂的白眼、
失恋的痛楚、法律的延宕、
衙门的傲慢、仁厚君子
所承受的无良小人的践踏,
要是用一柄出鞘的匕首,就可以
自行了断?有谁甘愿忍辱负重,

威廉·莎士比亚 William Shakespeare

驮着疲惫的生命而呻吟流汗，
要不是因为对死后冥事的恐惧，
对那从未有人能去而复返的
神秘地界的恐惧，困扰了意志，
使我们宁愿忍受眼前的苦难，
而不敢纵身跃向未知的灾祸？
就这样，顾虑把我们全变成了懦夫，
也就这样，决断力的本色，
被思虑蒙上了一层病态的惨白，
蓄势待发的磅礴大业
也因为这层考量而流向走偏，
丧失了行动的名分。

【译者记】对于莎翁此作，拙译有一些不同于传统译本的理解。如原文"that is the question"：朱生豪译"一个"和"值得考虑"皆无出处，卞之琳译"这是问题"生硬而难达意，二者都忽略了定冠词"the"的作用；又如"by opposing end them"：若以朱译"把他们扫清"，或卞译"扫它个干净"，而不冒着豁出去归同于尽的决绝，何来"To be, or not to be"，或"To die, to sleep"之虞？因而"opposing"一词应另有含意；再如"patient merit of th' unworthy"：这里有"patient merit"（耐受之品德）和"th' unworthy"（卑劣者），吾不知朱译"费尽辛勤所换来"和卞译"埋头苦干的大才"竟自何而来。如此诸等，故有吾译。

威廉·莎士比亚 William Shakespeare

"To Be or Not to Be"

(Hamlet's Soliloquy)

To be, or not to be: that is the question:
Whether 'tis nobler in the mind to suffer
The slings and arrows of outrageous fortune,
Or to take arms against a sea of troubles,
And by opposing end them. To die, to sleep—
No more, and by a sleep to say we end
The heart-ache and the thousand natural shocks
That flesh is heir to; 'tis a consummation
Devoutly to be wish'd. To die, to sleep—
To sleep, perchance to dream—ay, there's the rub,
For in that sleep of death what dreams may come,
When we have shuffled off this mortal coil,
Must give us pause; there's the respect
That makes calamity of so long life:
For who would bear the whips and scorns of time,
Th' oppressor's wrong, the proud man's contumely,
The pangs of despis'd love, the law's delay,
The insolence of office, and the spurns
That patient merit of th' unworthy takes,
When he himself might his quietus make
With a bare bodkin; who would fardels bear,
To grunt and sweat under a weary life,
But that the dread of something after death,
The undiscover'd country from whose bourn

威廉·莎士比亚 William Shakespeare

No traveller returns, puzzles the will,
And makes us rather bear those ills we have
Than fly to others that we know not of?
Thus conscience does make cowards of us all;
And thus the native hue of resolution
Is sicklied o'er with the pale cast of thought,
And enterprises of great pitch and moment
With this regard their currents turn awry,
And lose the name of action.

约翰·邓恩
John Donne (1572–1631)

神圣商赖体之十

（商籁体）

死神你且别骄狂，尽管有人说
你强悍而可怖，你实在谈不上，
你自以为你已经打倒的对方，
其实不死，可怜你也杀不死我。
休息睡眠——你的外表无非这个，
从中定会流出许许多多欢愉，
一旦英豪离开我们随你而去，
尸骨即便安息灵魂将获解脱。
你被命运、机缘、暴帝、疯徒奴役，
你跟毒药、战争、疾病混作一团，
罂粟魔魅一样能送我们入眠，
更胜你那两下；你还有何得意？
睡眠一忽即逝，我们永将苏醒，
死亡将不存在；死神，你将死定。

约翰·邓恩 John Donne

（七律体）

死神且莫逞骄狂，
恐怖虚名未可当。
索命焉知人便逝，
劫生怎奈我难伤。
蚕眠即是阴曹影，
睡梦无非快意长。
但使英豪随尔去，
身休且喜彼魂翔。

尔为奴婢天为主，
暴帝疯徒皆汝王，
疾病战争居尔上，
毒罂迷咒共君床。
凡能致寐不相让，
何事死神凭自狂？
吾辈暂眠千古醒，
死神将死死将亡。

约翰·邓恩 John Donne

Holy Sonnet X

Death be not proud, though some have called thee
Mighty and dreadfull, for, thou art not soe,
For, those, whom thou think'st, thou dost overthrow,
Die not, poore death, nor yet canst thou kill mee.
From rest and sleepe, which but thy pictures bee,
Much pleasure, then from thee, much more must flow,
And soonest our best men with thee doe goe,
Rest of their bones, and souls deliverie.
Thou art slave to Fate, Chance, kings, and desperate men,
And dost with poyson, warre, and sicknesse dwell,
And poppie, or charmes can make us sleepe as well,
And better than thy stroake; why swell'st thou then?
One short sleepe past, wee wake eternally,
And death shall be no more; death, thou shalt die.

安德鲁·马维尔
Andrew Marvell (1621–1678)

致他的忸怩女友

咱若天地够宽,时间够多,
小姐,这忸怩就不算罪过。
咱俩就能坐下左思右顾,
到哪整天浪漫去轧马路。
您就置身印度恒河岸边,
把那红色宝石悠然寻捡:
我在亨伯河口望潮埋怨。
灭世洪水来前爱你十年,
你自回绝此情,随你乐意,
直到犹太信徒改宗皈依。
我的痴钝爱情延延增长,
比那悠悠帝国更慢更广;
花一百年赞美你那眼睛,
凝视你的额头目不转睛;
花两百年倾慕每只酥胸,
献给玉体他处三万秋冬;
至少一世欣赏每段妙身,

安德鲁·马维尔 Andrew Marvell

最后一世打开你那芳心。
小姐,你真当得如此崇拜,
我也绝然不会降格献爱。
　　可是在我背后我总听见
时间战车插翅逼近眼前;
况且在咱前方远处横卧
无穷无尽是那永恒沙漠。
你将美貌不再容颜尽丧;
石穴之中我歌不再回响;
彼时各色蛆虫将会试新
你那长久保全处子之身,
你的雅誉清名化作土屑,
我的全身情欲灰飞烟灭;
墓穴这般去处隐秘美妙,
可是我想没人在那拥抱。
　　因而,如今趁着青春秀色
晨露一般把你肌肤润泽,
趁着春心激情随时发动,
直如烈火涌出每个毛孔,
咱就及时行乐莫负光阴,
即刻欢爱像那怀春猛禽,
宁愿一口吞食二人时光,
不让时光咀嚼衰成枯秧。

安德鲁·马维尔 Andrew Marvell

且把全身活力全部甜蜜
揉作一个圆球不分我你,
扯着咱的欢乐猛烈奋争,
冲破生命途中铁门层层:
如此,虽然无计喝停太阳,
咱却能让太阳奔跑发光。

安德鲁·马维尔 Andrew Marvell

To His Coy Mistress

Had we but world enough, and time,
This coyness, lady, were no crime.
We would sit down, and think which way
To walk, and pass our long love's day.
Thou by the Indian Ganges' side
Shouldst rubies find; I by the tide
Of Humber would complain. I would
Love you ten years before the Flood,
And you should, if you please, refuse
Till the conversion of the Jews.
My vegetable love should grow
Vaster than empires and more slow;
An hundred years should go to praise
Thine eyes, and on thy forehead gaze;
Two hundred to adore each breast,
But thirty thousand to the rest;
An age at least to every part,
And the last age should show your heart.
For, lady, you deserve this state,
Nor would I love at lower rate.
      But at my back I always hear
Time's wingèd chariot hurrying near;
And yonder all before us lie
Deserts of vast eternity.
Thy beauty shall no more be found;
Nor, in thy marble vault, shall sound

安德鲁·马维尔 Andrew Marvell

My echoing song; then worms shall try
That long-preserved virginity,
And your quaint honour turn to dust,
And into ashes all my lust;
The grave's a fine and private place,
But none, I think, do there embrace.
    Now therefore, while the youthful hue
Sits on thy skin like morning dew,
And while thy willing soul transpires
At every pore with instant fires,
Now let us sport us while we may,
And now, like amorous birds of prey,
Rather at once our time devour
Than languish in his slow-chapped power.
Let us roll all our strength and all
Our sweetness up into one ball,
And tear our pleasures with rough strife
Through the iron gates of life:
Thus, though we cannot make our sun
Stand still, yet we will make him run.

亚历山大·蒲伯
Alexander Pope (1688–1744)

独居赋

(原体版)

乐哉此叟无奢冀,
心系家传几亩田,
惬意呼吸乡里气,
　足立自家园。

自家牛奶自家谷,
自产羊毛做裤衫,
家树绿荫消夏暑,
　柴木御冬寒。

置身时外为福幸,
岁月悠悠看逝川,
身健体康心底静,
　日默夜酣眠。

读书间憩悠闲客,

亚历山大·蒲伯 Alexander Pope

娱乐怡情意趣宽,
抱朴持真最快乐,
　沉思心自安。

但愿无闻生若杳,
惟期无泣死如然;
悄声离世无人晓,
　无碑识长眠。

（七绝版）

怡哉此叟无奢冀,
心系家传几亩田,
惬意呼吸乡里气,
舒心站立自家园。

自家牛奶自家谷,
自产羊毛做裤衫,
夏避树林消酷暑,
冬收柴木御严寒。

置身时外为福幸,
岁月悠悠看逝川,
身健体康心底静,
日间少语夜酣眠。

亚历山大·蒲伯 Alexander Pope

读书间憩有余闲，
娱乐怡情意趣宽，
抱朴持真称惬快，
沉思默想心神安。

但愿无闻生若杳，
惟期无泣死如然；
悄声离世无人晓，
不立石碑识长眠。

【译者记】1、原诗每节前三行为四步抑扬格，末行为二步抑扬格，节奏有类"三句半"，却略呈宋词意味。拙译"原体版"模拟其体，并依原韵式，而持一韵到底。
2、拙译"七绝版"每节采用七绝格律，一韵到底，时而得以兼顾原诗韵式，或也另有意趣？

亚历山大·蒲伯 Alexander Pope

Ode on Solitude

Happy the man, whose wish and care
A few paternal acres bound,
Content to breathe his native air,
In his own ground.

Whose herds with milk, whose fields with bread,
Whose flocks supply him with attire,
Whose trees in summer yield him shade,
In winter fire.

Blest! who can unconcern'dly find
Hours, days, and years slide soft away,
In health of body, peace of mind,
Quiet by day,

Sound sleep by night; study and ease
Together mix'd; sweet recreation,
And innocence, which most does please,
With meditation.

Thus let me live, unseen, unknown;
Thus unlamented let me die;
Steal from the world, and not a stone
Tell where I lie.

奥利弗·哥尔德史密斯
Oliver Goldsmith (1728–1774)

当可爱的女人失足犯傻[a]

当可爱的女人失足犯傻,
发现男人负心已来不及,
安抚她的忧伤有何魔法?
洗去她的眼泪有何妙计?

唯此招术能够掩盖过错,
将她的羞辱在人前藏起,
能让她那情人悔恨思过,
并绞痛他肝肠,那便是——死。

---

[a] 此诗取自哥尔德斯密斯(Goldsmith)《威克菲尔德的牧师》中第二十四章,奥莉维亚回到自己被诱奸之地时所唱的歌。

奥利弗·哥尔德史密斯 Oliver Goldsmith

When Lovely Woman Stoops to Folly

When lovely woman stoops to folly,
And finds too late that men betray,
What charm can soothe her melancholy?
What art can wash her tears away?

The only art her guilt to cover,
To hide her shame from ev'ry eye,
To give repentance to her lover,
And wring his bosom is—to die.

安娜·拉埃蒂茨娅·巴鲍德
Anna Laetitia Barbauld (1743–1825)

生命若何我不知

那迷人的小魂灵,正急驰而去。

生命若何我不知,
唯知君我有别时;
何年何地缘何会,
自愧于今未解识。

但知生命既归西,
身首任凭何处栖,
余体残渣无所益,
不值石土不值泥。

敢问君将何处飞?
无痕路径有曲回?
此别奇异无他请,
谓我何方觅骨灰?

高天净火浩如洋,
生命于斯始肇祥,

安娜·拉埃蒂茨娅·巴鲍德 Anna Laetitia Barbauld

一旦弃尘脱阻绊，
君将飞返至天堂？

君或藏身暂隐形，
宛如骑士陷迷情，
经年漫度依期醒，
破梦重回力再生？

其间可有情思无？
君不为君君何如？

欣逢生命长相伴，
共享阳光共霭烟；
挚友作别情可叹，
疑将洒泪意何堪；

君退何妨择退日，
人无相扰去无言；
无为入夜说珍重，
晴日劳君道早安。

【译者记】此诗首段节奏工整，四步双行韵，而后二段转成为长短句。拙译采用七绝之格。虽然也曾试译为长短句而循原韵式，终未献丑于此。

安娜·拉埃蒂茨娅·巴鲍德 Anna Laetitia Barbauld

Life! I Know Not What Thou Art

Animula, vagula, blandula.

LIFE! I know not what thou art,
But know that thou and I must part;
And when, or how, or where we met,
I own to me 's a secret yet.
But this I know, when thou art fled,
Where'er they lay these limbs, this head,
No clod so valueless shall be
As all that then remains of me.
O whither, whither dost thou fly?
Where bend unseen thy trackless course?
And in this strange divorce,
Ah, tell where I must seek this compound I?

To the vast ocean of empyreal flame
From whence thy essence came
Dost thou thy flight pursue, when freed
From matter's base encumbering weed?
Or dost thou, hid from sight,
Wait, like some spell-bound knight,
Through blank oblivious years th' appointed hour
To break thy trance and reassume thy power?
Yet canst thou without thought or feeling be?
O say, what art thou, when no more thou'rt thee?

安娜·拉埃蒂茨娅·巴鲍德 Anna Laetitia Barbauld

Life! we have been long together,
Through pleasant and through cloudy weather;
'Tis hard to part when friends are dear;
Perhaps 'twill cost a sigh, a tear;
Then steal away, give little warning,
Choose thine own time;
Say not Good-night, but in some brighter clime
Bid me Good-morning!

威廉·布莱克
William Blake (1757–1827)

啊！向阳花

啊向阳花，你厌倦了时光，
细数着太阳缓缓的脚步，
追寻那美妙的金色阳光
那旅人行程终结的国度；

那里欲望少年憔悴而亡，
苍白处子裹着雪的尸布，
他们从墓中爬起来，神往
我那向阳花追寻的国度！

威廉·布莱克 William Blake

Ah! Sun-flower

Ah Sunflower, weary of time,
Who countest the steps of the sun:
Seeking after that sweet golden clime
Where the traveller's journey is done;

Where the Youth pined away with desire,
And the pale virgin shrouded in snow:
Arise from their graves and aspire,
Where my Sunflower wishes to go!

威廉·布莱克 William Blake

永恒

（九言体）

谁若独自占有那精灵，
他将毁灭带翅的生命；
谁亲吻那精灵任它飞，
他将沐浴永恒的朝辉。

（七言体）

君爱美兮君缚之
羽翅生灵君毁之
君吻美兮君由之
永恒朝日君居之

（五言体）

爱美囚于室
生灵折羽翅
吻之凭美飞
旭日永恒赐[a]

---

[a] 永恒：原文大写的"Eternity"是古典哲学和宗教概念。

威廉·布莱克 William Blake

Eternity

He who binds to himself a joy
Does the winged life destroy;
But he who kisses the joy as it flies
Lives in Eternity's sunrise.

威廉·华兹华斯
William Wordsworth (1770–1850)

草的辉煌

何患那曾经亮丽的容光
在眼前被夺走永远消亡,
何患那个时辰一去不再——
那草的辉煌,那花的光彩;
我们不会悲伤,我们寻找力量
在那仍然存留的宝藏:
那与生具来的同感之心——
它自古有之也必将永存;
那温暖人心的关切之情——
它是人生苦难的结晶;
那看穿死亡的信仰,
那带来哲思的年年岁岁。

【译者记】"草的辉煌"是诗人《颂诗:忆童年而悟永生》第十首中后部的12行,采用古希腊抒情诗人品达罗斯颂歌体,每行长度不定,韵法约可表达为:AABBCCDDEEFG,译文照搬。

威威廉·华兹华斯 William Wordsworth

Splendour in the Grass

What though the radiance which was once so bright
Be now for ever taken from my sight,
   Though nothing can bring back the hour
Of splendour in the grass, of glory in the flower;
      We will grieve not, rather find
      Strength in what remains behind;
      In the primal sympathy
      Which having been must ever be;
      In the soothing thoughts that spring
      Out of human suffering;
      In the faith that looks through death,
In years that bring the philosophic mind.

威威廉·华兹华斯 William Wordsworth

独荡似闲云

（五言体，原韵式）

独荡似闲云，
漂游丘壑间。
忽逢一大群，
灿灿金水仙；
湖畔树荫立，
随风舞曳曳。

连绵比银河，
闪烁如星汉。
沿岸长延拓，
盈湾无间断。
一望万千朵，
仰首舞婀娜。

近边波浪舞，
花跃更翩翩。
幸有花为伍，
诗人岂不欢。
花开足可贵，
凝望未曾会：

威威廉·华兹华斯 William Wordsworth

每每倚床前，
空思或默想，
心中现水仙，
独处惟能享。
起舞我心欢，
翩然伴水仙。

我独自游荡像一片闲云

（自由体，原韵式）

我独自游荡像一片闲云，
飘越在峡谷和山峦。
倏然我看到成簇成群，
一大片金灿灿的水仙；
在湖边，在树底，
随风起舞摇摇曳曳。

水仙延绵像星星闪烁
在那银河中眨着眼，
花海无间断地展拓，
沿着湖湾的堤岸：

威威廉·华兹华斯 William Wordsworth

一眼望去千朵万朵，
点头舞蹈轻盈婀娜。

近边的水浪也在起舞；
而花的舞蹈更为翩翩：
能与快乐的水仙为伍，
诗人无法不愉悦心欢：
凝望良久却未能体会
花展的馈赠多么珍贵：

我常常倚在床榻之前，
空无一念或沉思静默，
它们便闪现在我心田，
那是独居才有的欢乐；
愉悦便把我内心充满，
我也起舞陪伴那水仙。

【译者记】原作格式为四步抑扬格，每阕韵式为 ABABCC。

威威廉·华兹华斯 William Wordsworth

I Wandered Lonely as a Cloud

I wandered lonely as a cloud
That floats on high o'er vales and hills,
When all at once I saw a crowd,
A host, of golden daffodils;
Beside the lake, beneath the trees,
Fluttering and dancing in the breeze.

Continuous as the stars that shine
And twinkle on the milky way,
They stretched in never-ending line
Along the margin of a bay:
Ten thousand saw I at a glance,
Tossing their heads in sprightly dance.

The waves beside them danced; but they
Out-did the sparkling waves in glee:
A poet could not but be gay,
In such a jocund company:
I gazed—and gazed—but little thought
What wealth the show to me had brought:

For oft, when on my couch I lie
In vacant or in pensive mood,
They flash upon that inward eye
Which is the bliss of solitude;
And then my heart with pleasure fills,
And dances with the daffodils.

威威廉·华兹华斯 William Wordsworth

作于西敏寺桥上

（原韵式）

大地无法奉上更美景象：
心灵痴钝才会视而不见
雄伟辉煌如此动人景观：
这座城市穿起绚丽衣裳

是那晨的美丽：宁静和祥，
航船、教堂、拱顶、剧场、塔尖
铺展开来，面向大地长天，
在如洗的晴空熠熠闪光。

太阳从未用它首缕晨晖
如此浸染峡谷、岩石、山岗：
从未见过宁静如此深邃！

河水随心所欲缓缓流淌：
天啊！座座屋宇像在沉睡；
如此宁静是这伟大心脏！

威威廉·华兹华斯 William Wordsworth

（单韵）

世上再美不过这般景象：
心灵痴钝才会错失欣赏
美景如此动人雄伟辉煌：
这座城市穿起绚丽衣裳

是那晨的美丽：宁静和祥，
航船尖塔拱顶剧场教堂
面向大地长天展开臂膀，
在如洗的晴空熠熠闪光。

太阳从未将其首缕阳光
如此浸染峡谷岩石山岗：
宁静深邃是我前所未享！

河水随心所欲舒缓流淌；
天啊！座座屋宇沉睡一样；
静如处子是这伟大心脏！

【译者记】两个译本采用不同的韵法，即原文十四行诗的韵式和中文较习惯的韵法，或可比较二者韵律感觉的异同。前一译本有半押韵者，未能细究。

威威廉·华兹华斯 William Wordsworth

Composed upon Westminster Bridge

Earth has not anything to show more fair:
Dull would he be of soul who could pass by
A sight so touching in its majesty:
This City now doth like a garment wear

The beauty of the morning: silent, bare,
Ships, towers, domes, theatres, and temples lie
Open unto the fields, and to the sky,
All bright and glittering in the smokeless air.

Never did sun more beautifully steep
In his first splendour valley, rock, or hill;
Ne'er saw I, never felt, a calm so deep!

The river glideth at his own sweet will:
Dear God! the very houses seem asleep;
And all that mighty heart is lying still!

拉尔夫·沃尔多·爱默生
Ralph Waldo Emerson (1803–1882)

紫杜鹃
——答问花自何方来

五月海风破寂寥,
林中喜见杜鹃娆,
花放满枝幽境栖,
欢娱荒漠悦缓溪。
紫瓣飘飘坠碧池,
幽水欣欣凭落英;
红雀或来凉羽翅,
愧色向花诉衷情。
若有圣贤问杜鹃,
焉弃芳容天地间,
答之生眼为睛明,
丽质当因丽质生;
堪比玫瑰焉落此?
未曾自问未曾晓;
若依浅见试猜思,
君来我至皆天道。

拉尔夫·沃尔多·爱默生 Ralph Waldo Emerson

The Rhodora

On Being Asked, Whence Is The Flower?

In May, when sea-winds pierced our solitudes,
I found the fresh Rhodora in the woods,
Spreading its leafless blooms in a damp nook,
To please the desert and the sluggish brook.
The purple petals, fallen in the pool,
Made the black water with their beauty gay;
Here might the red-bird come his plumes to cool,
And court the flower that cheapens his array.
Rhodora! if the sages ask thee why
This charm is wasted on the earth and sky,
Tell them, dear, that if eyes were made for seeing,
Then Beauty is its own excuse for being:
Why thou wert there, O rival of the rose!
I never thought to ask, I never knew:
But, in my simple ignorance, suppose
The self-same Power that brought me there brought you.

【译者记】原诗五步抑扬格，AABB CDCD EEFF GHGH，似为商籁体之拓展，措辞古雅。故仿古风，而依原韵式迻译。

艾米莉·狄金森
Emily Dickinson (1830–1886)

未能停步等死神

未能停步等死神—
死神为我停—
车上唯有我两人—
永生也同行。

我们驾车缓缓行—
死神并不急,
我弃劳作与悠闲,
因他颇有礼—

走过校园—是课间
学童竞游戏—
走过**谷**穗满田间—
走过日落西—

或说太阳走过我—
露珠颤颤凉—
我袍轻薄如蝉翼—
披肩如绢网—

艾米莉·狄金森 Emily Dickinson

车停一幢房屋前
它像地隆起—
房顶无形难得见—
房檐埋入地—

自此—世纪虽更替
仿佛刚过晌
首次想到马头前
永恒是方向—

Because I could not stop for Death

Because I could not stop for Death –
He kindly stopped for me –
The Carriage held but just Ourselves –
And Immortality.

We slowly drove – He knew no haste
And I had put away
My labor and my leisure too,
For His Civility –

We passed the School, where Children strove
At Recess – in the Ring –

艾米莉·狄金森 Emily Dickinson

We passed the Fields of Gazing Grain –
We passed the Setting Sun –

Or rather – He passed us –
The Dews drew quivering and chill –
For only Gossamer, my Gown –
My Tippet – only Tulle –

We paused before a House that seemed
A Swelling of the Ground –
The Roof was scarcely visible –
The Cornice – in the Ground –

Since then – 'tis Centuries – and yet
Feels shorter than the Day
I first surmised the Horses' Heads
Were toward Eternity –

威廉·巴特勒·叶芝

William Butler Yeats (1865-1939)

二次降临

盘旋盘旋，螺旋中越旋越远
猎鹰听不到主人的招唤；
事态崩溃；中心无法撑持；
彻底的混乱放逐到世间，
血污的大潮肆虐，所到之处
吞没了崇尚纯真的仪典；
至善者缺乏信念，至恶者
却是神经亢奋，激情满满。

该是某种启示就在眼前；
该是二次降临就在眼前。
二次降临！未等这话出口
全球魂灵一个巨大幻象[a]
迷惑了我的眼：大漠之中
那形体长着狮身和人面，
那凝视无情如白日一般，

---

[a] "全球魂灵"译自拉丁文"Spiritus Mundi"，字面直解为世界之灵魂，此处代表某个时代的精神世界和社会价值，或曰一种集体无意识。

威廉·巴特勒·叶芝 William Butler Yeats

挪动着迟滞的双腿，周遭
沙漠飞禽的阴影在怒卷。
黑暗再次落下；我才醒悟
两千年那顽石般的沉睡
被晃动的摇篮搅成梦魇，
那是什么凶兽，时辰终至
缓缓挪向伯利恆去降生？

【译者记】作为无韵诗（blank verse），此作采用抑扬五步之格，而未用韵（第二段首两行视作重复）。译文选择用韵，一则押韵较为易行，二则顺势押韵以替换较难调整的节奏，以期在总体上约略等值地对应原文格律。未知如此处理能否获得一些认同。

威廉·巴特勒·叶芝 William Butler Yeats

The Second Coming

Turning and turning in the widening gyre
The falcon cannot hear the falconer;
Things fall apart; the centre cannot hold;
Mere anarchy is loosed upon the world,
The blood-dimmed tide is loosed, and everywhere
The ceremony of innocence is drowned;
The best lack all conviction, while the worst
Are full of passionate intensity.

Surely some revelation is at hand;
Surely the Second Coming is at hand.
The Second Coming! Hardly are those words out
When a vast image out of *Spiritus Mundi*
Troubles my sight: somewhere in sands of the desert
A shape with lion body and the head of a man,
A gaze blank and pitiless as the sun,
Is moving its slow thighs, while all about it
Reel shadows of the indignant desert birds.
The darkness drops again; but now I know
That twenty centuries of stony sleep
Were vexed to nightmare by a rocking cradle,
And what rough beast, its hour come round at last,
Slouches towards Bethlehem to be born?

威廉·巴特勒·叶芝 William Butler Yeats

智慧随着时光而来

树叶虽多根一只；
常思年少虚妄时，
阳光之下花枝俏；
今将枯萎入平实。

【译者记】此诗不同于中国韵律诗之处，在于不是每两行构成一个稳定的结构，而是第一行单独成意，而第二行跟第三、四行成为一体；类似的例子还有莎翁的"商籁体之六十六"等。如此，尽管造成译文读起来有行间失衡之感，亦不便轻易改动。

The Coming Of Wisdom With Time

Though leaves are many, the root is one;
Through all the lying days of my youth
I swayed my leaves and flowers in the sun;
Now I may wither into the truth.

沃尔特·萨维奇·兰德
Walter Savage Landor (1775–1864)

一世无争

（七绝版）

一世无争不屑争；
自然吾爱艺吾情。
人生火暖温双手，
火萎何辞踏去程。

（五律版）

从未与人斗，无人值我争。
自然吾挚爱，艺术我真情。
生命火曾旺，火温伴我行；
而今火既萎，何吝踏归程。

【译者记】诗人此诗，常被称作"哲人遗言"，意在总结一生，用的是过去时态。尤其第一行声称自己从未与人争斗，

沃尔特·萨维奇·兰德 Walter Savage Landor

而非表明不与人争斗的姿态；且原诗读来虽轻散，却格律甚整，采用五步抑扬格，ABAB 韵法，而绝非自由体诗。流传多个译本，各抒胸臆，而忽略了此诗的内涵和格律。试呈七绝五律二个译本，前者亦可于首行改一字作"一世无争不屑斗"，而合原韵式。

（另，诗人自诩归自诩，其用意是否认；事实上他却堪称一位"争气机"，时时处处跟人起争端。对照其作品，不是很有趣味吗？）

I Strove with None

I strove with none, for none was worth my strife;
Nature I loved, and next to Nature, Art;
I warmed both hands before the fire of Life;
It sinks, and I am ready to depart.

埃兹拉·庞德

Ezra Pound (1885–1972)

致意

哦,你们这十足自鸣得意
却又十足缺乏自在的一代,
我见过渔翁在阳光下野餐,
见过他们带着邋遢的家人,
我见过他们满口露齿的笑容
听过他们狂浪的笑声。
因而我比你们幸福,
而他们比我更幸福;
你看那鱼儿在湖中游
它们连衣服都没有。

埃兹拉·庞德 Ezra Pound

Salutation

O generation of the thoroughly smug
and thoroughly uncomfortable,
I have seen fishermen picnicking in the sun,
I have seen them with untidy families,
I have seen their smiles full of teeth
and heard ungainly laughter.
And I am happier than you are,
And they were happier than I am;
And the fish swim in the lake
and do not even own clothing.

托马斯·斯特恩斯·艾略特
Thomas Stearns Eliot (1888–1965)

荒 原[1]

"因我曾亲眼看见库迈的西比拉吊在一只罐子里,当孩子们问她'西比拉,你想要咋样?'她回答,'我想死。'"[a]

献给埃兹拉·庞德
艺高一筹[b]

一、葬亡

四月之月最是残酷,把
丁香在那死地上滋育,把

---

[a] 原文为拉丁文夹希腊文,出自一世纪小说家盖厄斯·佩特罗尼乌斯·阿尔比特作品《萨蒂里孔》中的人物 Encolpius 之口:"NAM sibyllam quidem Cuimis ego ipse oculis meis vidi in ampulla pendere, et cum illi pueri dicerent: Σιβνλλατιθελειζ; repondebat illa: αποθαν ειν θελω." 西比拉即女先知,而库迈的西比拉 是希腊神话中最有名的女先知。她得到阿波罗的恩赐,可享如一抔土中的颗粒数那样的长寿,却未能得到青春,故于老朽之年渴求死亡。

　　另,英文原诗中出现的外文,无论在原文中是否以斜体出现,译本都用楷体表示;所有脚注均为译者所加,以字母标注;诗人原作尾注在译文中仍作尾注,增加数字标注,必要处在原注后附译者记,提供详情或解释。
[b] 原文为意大利文:"il miglior fabbro"(引自但丁《神曲·炼狱篇》第26首)。

托马斯·斯特恩斯·艾略特 Thomas Stearns Eliot

记忆和欲望搅作一团，把

麻木的根用春雨拨弄。

5　冬天保了我们温暖，把

大地盖上忘世的雪，把

一丝生机用枯茎喂养。[a]

夏天给了我们一惊，掠过施塔恩贝格湖

携雨而至；我们在柱廊里稍候，

10　接着在阳光下，走进王宫花园，[b]

喝着咖啡，聊了一个小时。

我可不是俄罗斯人，我来自立陶宛，正宗日耳曼人[c]

我们小时候，在大公家小住，[d]

就是表兄家，他带我去滑雪橇，

15　我很害怕。他说，玛丽，

玛丽，手抓牢啊。我们便一冲而下。

在大山里，真是自由自在。

我读书读个大半夜，冬天就去南方。

---

[a] 参见詹姆士·汤姆森（James Thomson）《致死亡诸女神》（*To Our Ladies of Death*）中的诗句："母亲养育了我们幼小的生命，使我们能以死反哺于她。"

[b] 施塔恩贝格湖：慕尼黑南面一片湖，巴伐利亚国王同性恋者路德维希二世的尸体于湖中找到；王宫花园：慕尼黑城内一座公园。

[c] 原文为德文："Bin gar keine Russin, stamm' aus Litauen, echt deutsch"，在原诗中没有用斜体。其中"Russin"是阴性，表明叙述者是女性，人物原型当是玛丽·路易斯·拉里施伯爵夫人，即第 15 行中的"玛丽"，艾略特称曾与她会面。这一段的情节与拉里施伯爵夫人的回忆录《我的过去》（*My Past*）中的叙述相吻合。

[d] 大公：可能指奥匈帝国皇储鲁道夫，因婚姻不幸，精神崩溃，与情妇一同自杀身亡；或指皇储弗朗茨·斐迪南大公，在萨拉热窝被塞尔维亚王国民族主义者普林西普刺杀身亡，成为第一次世界大战的导火线。

托马斯·斯特恩斯·艾略特 Thomas Stearns Eliot

是什么根紧抓这烂石堆，什么枝ᵃ
20 从这烂石堆中长出来？人子啊，²
你说不出，猜不到，因为你所见只是
一堆破碎景象，那里烈日暴晒，
死树不给遮庇，蟋蟀不给宽慰，³
干石头不发出一丝水声。只是
25 这红色岩石之下才有庇荫，ᵇ
（来吧，钻进这红岩下的庇荫），
我要给你看一样东西，既不像
早晨在身后随你迈步的影子，
也不像傍晚升起迎你的影子；
30 我要给你看一抔尘土中的恐惧。ᶜ

清风习习地吹呀
吹到我家乡
我那爱尔兰姑娘呀
你流连在何方？⁴

35 "一年前你第一次送我风信子；

ᵃ 参阅《圣经·旧约·约伯记》第8章第17节："他的根盘绕石堆，钻入石缝。"
ᵇ 参阅《圣经·旧约·以赛亚书》第32章："必有一人像避风所，和避暴雨的隐密处，像干旱之地的溪水，又像疲乏之地的大盘石的阴影。"
ᶜ 一抔尘土：参见题词的脚注；另一说认为"一抔尘土"来自约翰·邓恩的《祈祷集》（*Devotions*）；第三种解释认为与英国国教葬亡祭词"尘归尘，土归土"相关。

托马斯·斯特恩斯·艾略特 Thomas Stearns Eliot

"他们都叫我风信子姑娘。"ᵃ
——可我们很晚从风信子园回来时,
你两臂满抱,湿着头发,我却说不
出话,眼睛也看不见,我既不
40 活又不死,什么也不知道,
凝望着光亮的深处,一片寂静。ᵇ
荒凉空寂是那大海。⁵

梭梭垂斯夫人,那有名的慧眼,ᶜ
患了重感冒,尽管如此
45 仍被认作欧洲最通神的女人,
手握一副诡妙的纸牌。这张,她说,⁶
是你的牌,淹死的腓尼基水手,ᵈ
(那些明珠原是他的眼睛。瞧啊!)ᵉ

ᵃ 风信子姑娘:希腊神话中阿波罗爱上斯巴达王的儿子海厄森斯(Hyacinth)却不幸导致他死亡,后以"风信子"纪念他,故传统上风信子代表美男子。这几行有两层含义:1.荒原之中,纯爱已死;2.影射男女不辨和变态性爱(这些在当时是不"正确"的)的无力无能。

ᵇ 从38行到41行的各个词句或情景皆出自但丁《神曲》《地狱篇》和《天堂篇》两篇的尾章,暗喻现代荒原中爱情的瘫痪及其被救赎的可能性。另,评者论"光亮的深处(heart of light)"或与约瑟夫·康拉德的heart of darkness有深层联系。

ᶜ 梭梭垂斯:由赫胥黎(Aldous Huxley)小说《铭黄》(*Crome Yellow*)中女巫师Sesostris的名字衍生而来。书中斯科根先生(Scogan)冒名Sesostris扮作吉普赛女巫师,在集市上算命。普遍认为其原型是哲学家伯特兰·罗素。赫胥黎与罗素多有交集,前者把他对后者的印象注入人物斯科根加以讽刺。

ᵈ 参见第四部分"溺亡"中的弗莱巴,联系下文"当心溺亡水中"。

ᵉ 见莎士比亚《暴风雨》第一幕第二场中爱丽儿唱的丧歌(朱生豪译):"五浔的水深处躺着你的父亲,他的骨骼已化成珊瑚;他眼睛是耀眼的明

托马斯·斯特恩斯·艾略特 Thomas Stearns Eliot

这张是贝拉东纳,岩间女士,ᵃ
50 那位随情就景的女士。
这张是持三根权杖者,这张是转轮,ᵇ
这张是独眼商人,而这张牌ᶜ
空白一张,是他背在背上
不让我看的。我找不到
55 那张倒悬者。当心溺亡水中。ᵈ
我看到成群的人,围成圈子走动。
谢谢。你若见到亲爱的艾奎通太太ᵉ
请告诉她我亲自带着星象图:
这年头是要格外谨慎的呀。

60 诡异的城啊,⁷
在冬日拂晓的褐色雾中,

珠;他消失的全身没有一处不曾受到海水神奇的变幻,化成瑰宝,富丽而珍怪。"

ᵃ "贝拉东纳(Belladonna)"一词源于意大利语 bella donna,意为"漂亮女人",是一种植物(颠茄),可制眼用化妆品,也是毒药,其中"donna"含圣母之意;"岩间女士(the Lady of the Rocks)"暗指达芬奇作品《岩间圣母》(*Virgin of the Rocks*)和《蒙娜丽莎》(*Mona Lisa*);在下一行又转成"那位随情就景的女士",综合起来,应该代表了诗中各种情景下的女性人物。参见原注第218行。

ᵇ "持三根权杖者":见原注第46行;转轮:即命运转轮。

ᶜ 独眼商人:即第三节"火诫"里贩卖葡萄干的尤金尼德斯先生。"独眼"是卡上的形象,暗示无良、罪恶或海盗。

ᵈ "倒悬者"与"雷之语"中"罩着头的人"相通。他象征丰产之神的自我牺牲,以便在重生之日为大地带来丰产。因为他"罩着头",所以梭梭垂斯夫人看不到他。

ᵉ 艾奎通太太:一说诗人用艾奎通代表他所讨厌的妻子薇薇恩。传闻罗素与薇薇恩有染,此处暗讽二人。参阅第43行脚注。

托马斯·斯特恩斯·艾略特 Thomas Stearns Eliot

一群人流过伦敦桥,那么多人,
没想到死神竟报废了那么多人。⁸
叹息,短促的叹息,偶而嘘出,⁹
65 每个人的眼睛都锁定在脚前。
流上街坡又流下威廉王大街,
流到圣玛丽·伍尔诺斯教堂^a
敲响九点钟最后沉死的一响。¹⁰
我看到一个熟人,喊住了他:"斯特森!^b
70 你,在迈利和我在一个舰队的!^c
去年你栽在花园里的尸体,^d
开始发芽了吗?今年会开花吗?
还是突来的霜冻惊扰了它的温床?^e
哦,把大犬弄远点,那是人的朋友,¹¹
75 不然它会用爪子把尸体再挖出来!
你!虚伪的读者!——我的同流——我的兄弟!"¹²

---

^a 圣玛丽·伍尔诺斯教堂位于"伦敦城"(即伦敦金融区),被"报废了"的现代人群按时按点"流"入该区上班。
^b "斯特森(Stetson)":其来源有几说:或艾略特银行同事的名字,或艾略特的朋友埃兹拉·庞德(常戴斯特森帽),或伦敦一家帽商的字号,因很多人戴这家商铺的帽子,因而泛指任何人。
^c 迈利:西西里一海港。公元前 260 年,罗马在迈利附近赢得对迦太基的重要海战。能遇见千年以前死亡战友的场所暗合但丁笔下的地狱,那里可以遇见亡魂。承接上文死亡的钟声将人带入地狱一样"诡异"的地方。
^d "尸体"的原文"corpse",另指巨花魔芋,俗称尸花。
^e "突来的霜冻惊扰了它的温床":这里一语三关,包含了苗、性和死。

托马斯·斯特恩斯·艾略特 Thomas Stearns Eliot

二、棋局

  她坐的椅子，像锃亮的御座，[13]
  在大理石地面熠熠生辉，镜子
  支在镂着果实藤蔓的框柱中
80 藤蔓中有个金色丘比特向外探望
  （另一个把眼睛藏在翅膀后面）
  将七枝烛台的火苗翻倍
  又把烛光反射到桌面，而
  她那珠宝的晶晶华光从富丽的
85 锦盒中升起，与烛光交相辉映；
  一个个象牙瓶和彩色玻璃瓶
  瓶盖开启，她那些合成香精，
  膏状，粉状，液态——怪味暗飘
  迷乱并淹没着嗅觉；窗口空气
90 清新袭来，一经搅动，气味上升，
  把细长的烛焰挑得粗壮，
  又把烛烟直甩到镶板顶棚间，[14]
  拂动着方格天花板上的图案。
  浸了铜盐的巨块海漂木[a]
95 燃出绿色和橙色，色彩映在石框上，
  那悲伤的火光中，游着一头雕刻的海豚。
  古旧的壁炉台上展示着
  犹如窗口展示着田野风光[15]

---

[a] 海漂木经海水浸泡后留在上面的铜盐燃烧时呈绿色。

一幅菲洛墨拉的变形，她被野蛮的国王[16]
100　所强暴；然而那夜莺却[17]
　　　用她凛然的呼声填满整个荒漠
　　　她恒定地在呼喊，而世界至今在驱赶，
　　　"啾啾"，对着肮脏的耳朵。
　　　还有些时光的残桩旧事
105　陈述在墙壁上；各种形体凝视着
　　　探出身，斜倚着，嘘静围起的空间。
　　　脚步声在楼梯上嚓嚓作响。
　　　火光下，发刷下，她的头发
　　　散发开像飞溅的点点火星
110　闪作话语，接着是一片死寂。

　　　"今夜我神经很糟。是，很糟。留下陪我。
　　　跟我说话。你为什么总不说话。说话呀。
　　　你在想什么？想什么？什么？
　　　我从来不知道你在想什么。想想吧。"

115　我想我们落到了鼠坑里，[18]
　　　死人丢弃了尸骨的地方。[a]

　　　"那是什么声音？"
　　　　　　是门底的风。[19]

---

[a] 这里的意象可能来自一战中士兵抛尸于老鼠成灾的战壕，暗含失去雄风和精神，还暗喻两人的婚姻现状。

托马斯·斯特恩斯·艾略特 Thomas Stearns Eliot

"那又是什么声音？风在干什么？"
120 　　　　什么都没有什么都没干。
　　　　　　　　　"那
你什么都不知道？什么都没看见？什么都
不记得吗？"

　　我记得
125 那些明珠原是他的眼睛。
　　"你是活着还是死了？你脑壳里啥也没有吗？"[20]
　　　　　　　可是
哦哦哦哦那莎士比黑亚式的拉格——[a]
多么雅致
130 多么机智
　　"这下我该怎么办呢？该干什么呢？"
　　"我就这个样子冲出去，浪荡街头[b]
披散着头发，像这样。明天又该怎么办？
我们到底还能干什么？"
135 　　　　　　十点钟供热水。
如果下雨，四点钟来一辆闭蓬车。
我们还要下一局棋，
撑着眼皮巴望那一声敲门。[21]

---

[a] 拉格：拉格泰姆，散拍音乐。这里指当年一首流行的拉格泰姆歌曲。艾略特在标题中用了"Shakespe*h*erian Rag"拼法，应是有意的。下面两行转引自曲中歌词"最为机智/非常雅致"。
[b] 那个年代(1922)披散着头发行走街头是妓女形象。比较原文"walk the street"与短语"walk the streets"。

托马斯·斯特恩斯·艾略特 Thomas Stearns Eliot

丽尔的丈夫退伍时，我说——
140　我毫不含糊，亲口对她说，
　　赶紧着到点了[a]
　　艾伯特要回来了，去把自己收拾利落点。
　　他一准想知道他给你做牙的钱
　　你都花到哪儿了。他给了，我在场的。
145　去把牙全拔了吧，丽尔，配一副像样的，
　　他说，真心说，我真没法看你。
　　我也没法看你，我说，想想可怜的艾伯特，
　　他当兵四年了，想好好快活一下，[b]
　　你要是不给他，有人会给的，我说。
150　哦，有么，她说。差不多吧，我说。
　　那我就知道该谢谁了，说着她直盯了我一眼。
　　赶紧着到点了
　　就算你不乐意，也将就些吧，我说。
　　别人能挑三拣四，你可没得挑。
155　要是艾伯特跑了，可别怪没人提醒你。
　　你也不嫌寒碜，我说，看着那么老相。
　　（她才三十一岁。）
　　有啥办法，她拉长了脸说，
　　都怪吃的那些药，打胎的，她说。
160　（她已经五次了，生小乔治差点送了命。）

---

[a] 酒吧关门时服务生催客离去的习惯用语。
[b] 四年指第一次世界大战的四年（1914-1918）。

托马斯·斯特恩斯·艾略特 Thomas Stearns Eliot

药房说没事，可我再也不像从前了。
你真是个大傻瓜，我说。
可要是艾伯特不让你安生，就是这样，我说，
不想生孩子你干嘛要结婚？
165 **赶紧着到点了**
哦，那个星期天艾伯特在家，弄了条热熏腿
他们请我到家去吃饭，趁热品尝美味——
赶紧着到点了
赶紧着到点了
170 晚安，比尔。晚安，露。晚安，梅。晚安。[a]
拜拜。晚安。晚安。
晚安，太太们，晚安，可爱的小姐们，晚安，晚安。[b]

三、火诫[c]

河的蓬帐已破：树叶的残指
抓了抓便沉入湿湿的河堤。风
175 掠过褐色大地，没人听见。美少女都已离去。
可爱的泰晤士河啊，你轻轻地流，等我唱完我的歌。[22]
河面不再漂浮着空瓶子、三明治纸、
丝手绢、硬纸盒、烟蒂头

---

[a] 注意原文170-171两行中"晚安"的拼法："Goonight"。
[b] 典出《哈姆雷特》第四幕第五场中奥菲莉亚临死前的告别："晚安，太太们；晚安，可爱的小姐们；晚安，晚安！"另，奥菲莉亚精神失常后手持花束溺亡，极可能与本诗中手持风信子的女孩和溺亡的腓尼基水手相暗合。
[c] 佛陀在《火诫》中劝告人们摈弃各种欲望之火，以期脱离轮回，达到涅槃。

托马斯·斯特恩斯·艾略特 Thomas Stearns Eliot

也没了夏夜的其他痕迹。美少女都已离去。
180 还有她们的朋友,城中大亨们的浪荡后人;
都已经离去,没有留下地址。
坐在莱蒙湖的水边,我哭了……a
可爱的泰晤士河啊,你轻轻地流,等我唱完我的歌,
可爱的泰晤士河啊,你轻轻地流,我话声不高语不多。
185 可是我听见在背后的寒风中b
白骨咔咔作响,咧笑咯咯出声。

一只老鼠轻轻穿过草丛
拖着黏湿的肚皮在岸上爬行
而那个冬日的傍晚,我正在
190 煤气厂背后呆滞的渠中垂钓
默想着我那兄王的海难
以及之前我父王的惨死。[23]
白尸裸露在低洼的湿地
遗骨散落在矮燥的阁楼,
195 只是被老鼠踢得作响,年复一年。
可是在背后我不时听见[24]
喇叭和马达的声响,春天这声响[25]

---

a 莱蒙湖(Leman)是瑞士洛桑人对日内瓦湖的称呼。艾略特在洛桑治病期间完成此诗的一部分。许多人认为这一行暗合《圣经·诗篇 137》:"坐在巴比伦的河边,我们哭了。"英文词"leman"旧指情妇。
b 见原注 196 行。

托马斯·斯特恩斯·艾略特 Thomas Stearns Eliot

将送斯维尼到波特太太身旁。ª

哦,月光闪闪把波特太太照 26

200 也把她的女儿照

她俩用苏打水洗双脚

哦那些童声,在穹顶中歌唱! 27

咕,咕,咕

啾啾,啾啾,啾啾 ᵇ

205 那样粗野地强暴。

忒鲁 ᶜ

诡异的城啊

在冬日正午的褐色雾中,

尤金尼德斯先生,那位士麦那商人

210 胡子拉碴,满满一口袋葡萄干 28

伦敦到岸价:见票即付,

操一口粗俗的法语邀请我

到坎农街酒店进午餐

ª 斯维尼是艾略特创造的粗野人物,出现在他的多首诗中;波特太太是开罗一家妓院的老鸨。她们母女被一战中的澳大利亚士兵编入拉格泰姆歌词里,下面三行即来自歌词,其猥亵程度已被艾略特弱化。

ᵇ 参看约翰·利利(John Lyly)剧作《坎帕斯佩》(*Campaspe*)中的歌:"什么鸟儿这样唱,然而又是这样哭?哦,是那被强暴的夜莺。啾啾,啾啾,忒鲁,她哭道。"

ᶜ 忒鲁:既是本诗 99 行中强奸了菲洛墨拉的色雷斯国王名字忒鲁斯(Tereus)的呼格 Tereu,也是伊丽莎白时期诗歌中夜莺所唱的歌里惯用的词,见上注,在英文中与 to rue 谐音。二者皆含谴责之意。

托马斯·斯特恩斯·艾略特 Thomas Stearns Eliot

随后到大都会度周末。a

215 那紫色黄昏时分，当眼和腰
从桌面抬起，当人型机器在等候
像出租车搏动着等候的时分，
我提瑞舍斯，瞎着眼，搏动在两性间，29
长着皱巴巴女人乳房的老汉，却能看到
220 那紫色黄昏时分，傍晚归家的时段，
招呼水手离海回家的时段，30
打字员茶点时间回家，清理早餐，
点着炉火，摆出食品罐罐。
窗外，领受着最后的阳光
225 岌岌可危地晾着她的连裤衣
沙发上堆着（夜里当作床）
长筒袜、拖鞋、背心和胸衣。
我提瑞舍斯，长着干巴奶子的老汉
觉察到这一幕，就预言了下文——
230 我也在等候那位预期的客人。
他来了，那个年轻轻的粉刺脸，
房产经纪的小职员，眼神颇为轻佻，
这个低微之人身上摆着的自信
宛若布雷德福暴发户头上的丝礼帽。b

---

a 大都会：英国海边度假胜地布莱顿的一家豪华连锁酒店，邀请到这里度周末有性暖昧意味。
b 布雷德福是英国约克郡的一个产业城，其羊毛业和纺织业一战期间造就了一批暴发户。

托马斯·斯特恩斯·艾略特 Thomas Stearns Eliot

235 此刻时机很合适，据他猜测，
饭已吃完但见她，无聊困乏，
探手探脚拉过来搂抱亲热，
虽未见她来相迎也没遭骂。
脸一红来心一横立刻进攻；
240 上下其手去摸索没遇抗拒；
他那虚荣不需要任何回应，
一厢情愿把冷漠当成乐意。
（而我提瑞舍斯，早已领受过
这沙发这床榻上演的所有；
245 我曾经在底比斯城墙下坐，[a]
也曾在最卑微的死人中走。）[b]
他再把那最后一吻施舍上，
便摸着去路，只见楼梯没照亮……

她转身对着镜子看了看，
250 把那离去的情人全忘掉；
大脑中半个念头忽一闪：
"既然已经完事：完事就好。"
当可爱的女人失足犯傻，[31]
再次独自在家踱步之际，
255 她机械地抬手抹平头发，

---

[a] 在索福克勒斯的悲剧《俄狄浦斯王》中，正是提瑞舍斯在底比斯城墙下的披露，让俄狄浦斯王得知自己未能逃脱杀父娶母的不幸命运。
[b] 提瑞舍斯虽然得享长寿，但终有一死，而他死后仍有知觉。荷马史诗《奥德赛》中，奥德修斯造访冥间时曾与他相遇。

托马斯·斯特恩斯·艾略特 Thomas Stearns Eliot

又放了张唱片给留声机。

"这音乐贴着水面掠过我身边"³²
穿过河岸街，沿维多利亚女王街直上。
伦敦城啊伦敦城，我时而能听见ª
260 泰晤士下街的一家酒肆旁，
一只曼陀林那悦耳的哀鸣
还有里面叽叽嘎嘎的语声
午间渔贩们在那里歇晌：那里
马格纳斯殉道堂的墙上³³
265 是爱奥尼亚式白底描金的莫名辉煌。

  河面上渗出³⁴
  油花和沥青
  画舫只只
  随着退潮漂荡
270   红帆
  大张
  顺着风，摇摆在沉重的桅杆上。
  画舫浪拍
  漂移的原木
275   流过多格斯岛
  直下格林尼治水域。
  喂呵啦啦 咧呀

ª "伦敦城"即 The City，指伦敦金融区。

托马斯·斯特恩斯·艾略特 Thomas Stearns Eliot

哇啦啦　咧呀啦啦ᵃ

伊丽莎白和莱斯特³⁵
280　击水的船桨
　　　船尾的形状
　　　像镀金的贝壳
　　　红色间着金黄
　　　轻快的水波
285　在两岸拍成细浪
　　　西南风
　　　带向下游
　　　响亮的钟声
　　　白色的塔楼
290　喂呵啦啦　咧呀
　　　哇啦啦　咧呀啦啦

　　　"来往的电车灰土土的树。
　　　海布里生我。里士满和基尤³⁶ᵇ
　　　毁我。到了里士满我抬起双膝
295　仰卧船板在窄窄的独木舟。"

ᵃ 这"啦啦"歌让人联想到瓦格纳《尼伯龙根的指环》（*Der Ring des Nibelungen*）系列中四部歌剧的第一部《莱茵的黄金》（*Das Rheingold*）和第四部《诸神的黄昏》（*Götterdämmerung*）中莱茵河女儿所唱的歌。她们唱了两遍副歌"喂呵啦啦　咧呀 哇啦啦　咧呀啦啦"，一遍"啦啦"。
ᵇ 海布里、里士满、基尤都是伦敦市郊住宅区。

托马斯·斯特恩斯·艾略特 Thomas Stearns Eliot

"我双脚踩在穆尔垓,心ª
却踩在我脚底。事情过后
他哭了。他许诺要'自新'。
我没说话。我能有啥怨和仇?"

300 "在马盖特的沙滩上。ᵇ
我头脑空空
什么联想都没有。
破裂的指甲满手的脏。ᶜ
我们这些卑微之人
305 无所求。"
啦啦

于是我来到迦太基[37]

烧呀烧呀烧呀烧呀[38]
主啊,您救我出来吧[39]
310 主啊,您救啊

烧呀

---

a 穆尔垓:伦敦东区的贫民区。
b 马盖特:英国东南滨海一处度假胜地,艾略特曾遵医嘱于1921年在此休养一个月。
c 从草稿上划掉的一行可以看出艾略特想象的脏手应是男人的手,即泰晤士女儿父兄之手。

托马斯·斯特恩斯·艾略特 Thomas Stearns Eliot

四、溺亡^a

腓尼基人弗莱巴,死了已经两星期,^b
忘掉了鸥鸟的鸣叫,深海的浪涌
也忘掉了盈利和亏损。
315 　　　　海底一股暗流
悄声剔净他的骨头。一浮一沉中
他穿过一生每个阶段穿过青春
陷入漩涡。
　　　　无论是不是犹太人
320 哦,你这位转动舵轮查看风向的,
想想弗莱巴,他曾和你一样高大英俊。

五、雷之语[40]

火炬映红汗淋淋的脸庞过后^c
果园那寒霜般的寂静过后^d
乱石之间历经的磨难

---

^a 埃兹拉·庞德让艾略特删掉了《溺亡》的前 82 行,其文字描述一个水手航海遇难的历程。
^b 这一段文字来自艾略特 1918 年所作法文诗《在餐馆》,两处大同小异。法文原作试译如下:"腓尼基人弗莱巴,溺亡已经十五天,/忘了鸥鸟的叫声,/忘了康沃尔海的浪涌/也忘了盈利和亏损和一货舱罐头:/一股洋流载他去远方,/把他带到前世的各个阶段。/试想吧,这么悲惨的命运;/然而,他也曾高大英俊。"
^c 参见《圣经·约翰福音》第 18 章:"犹大领了一队兵,以及祭司长和法利赛人的圣殿警卫,拿着灯笼、火把和兵器来到园里。"
^d 暗指客西马尼园,耶路撒冷的一个果园。按照新约圣经和基督教传统说法,耶稣被钉死在十字架上的前夜,和他的门徒在最后的晚餐之后前往此处祷告。从 322 行到 328 行指的是耶稣从被捕到受难的整个过程。

托马斯·斯特恩斯·艾略特 Thomas Stearns Eliot

325 监牢宫殿中的
　　 哭叫呼喊还有远山
　　 春雷的回响都过去之后
　　 那位曾经活着的已经死去
　　 我们曾经活着的正在死去
330 只在耐心等候

　　 这里没有水只有烂石头
　　 只有石头没有水只有沙土路
　　 土路头顶绕，绕在大山里
　　 山是石头山，山间没有水
335 要是能有水咱就停步把水喝
　　 身处烂石间不能停步或思索
　　 汗水已流干双脚陷沙土
　　 多么渴望石头之间能有水
　　 死山嘴里是龋齿滴水不会吐
340 不能站来不能躺坐也坐不住
　　 这山里就连安静也没有
　　 只会干打瘠雷不下雨
　　 这山里就连孤独也没有
　　 只有阴沉的赤脸在讥吼
345 发自泥裂破屋的门口
　　　　　　但愿能有水
　　　　没有烂石头
　　　　就算有石头

但愿也有水
也有水
350 有泉水
石头之间一汪水
哪怕只是一缕水声
不是知了
和枯草在歌唱
355 而是石头上的流水声
和松树上隐居鸫的歌声
滴答滴答答答答[41]
可就是没有水

那第三个人是谁，他总在你身边走？
360 我点人数时，只有你我在一起[42]
可当我抬头看前方那白色的路
总是另有一个人在你身边走
悄悄滑行裹着棕色斗篷，罩着头
我不知道那是男人还是女人
365 ——可那是谁呀他在你的另一头？

那是什么声音凄厉在空中[43]
可是慈母哀伤的喃喃声
那群罩着头的是什么人，蜂拥
在无尽的原野，跌撞在坼裂的大地
370 只有扁扁的地平线才是边缘

托马斯·斯特恩斯·艾略特 Thomas Stearns Eliot

  那是哪座城市在山的那边
  崩裂、重建、爆炸在紫色暮空
  城楼倒坍中
  亚力山大 雅典 耶路撒冷
375 维也纳 伦敦
  诡异啊

  一个女人绷紧她那黑色长发
  在那些琴弦上弄出嗦嗦音响
  婴儿脸的蝙蝠在紫色暮光下
380 发出呼啸，扇动着翅膀
  头朝下沿着污黑的墙壁爬行
  几座钟塔倒挂在空中
  鸣响着勾起怀想的报时钟声
  还有吟唱之声传出空池和枯井。[a]

385 在这群山环抱的残破山沟
  教堂四周那坍塌的坟墓上
  幽暗的月光下，荒草在歌唱
  那空空的教堂，只是风的家。[b]
  没有窗户，门在摇晃，
390 枯骨无以为害。

---

[a] 《旧约》中"池"和"井"是信仰的活水之源，这里空池和枯井则象征信仰的干涸。
[b] 指寻求圣杯的骑士来到凶险教堂前一无所见、只见荒芜的绝望一刻。空幻是对骑士的最后考验。

托马斯·斯特恩斯·艾略特 Thomas Stearns Eliot

只有一只雄鸡站在屋脊上
咯咯里咯,咯咯里咯^a
随着雷电一闪。接着一股湿风
带来了雨

395 恒河干瘪了,萎靡的树叶^b
等待着雨,而滚滚乌云
远远地聚集在喜马望山。^c
莽林猫腰蹲伏着,静默无声。
于是雷发话了
400 哒
哒塔:我们施予了什么?[44]
朋友啊,热血激荡着我的心
那顷刻间舍弃的非凡勇气
那一世审慎也无法撤回的勇气
405 借此,唯独借此,我们得以生存
那勇气,它不会在我们的讣告中
不会在蜘蛛善意覆盖的墓志铭里[45]
也不会在瘦律师在我们那空屋
所拆开的封条下
410 哒

---

^a 原文为法文"Co co rico co co rico"。公鸡叫声在法国也是胜利和自豪之声;表示恶魔将离去。这两行可能暗指《圣经·路加福音》耶稣对彼得所说的话:"今日鸡叫以先,你要三次不认我。"
^b 恒河:原文为人格化的"Ganga"一词,即印度教中的恒河女神。
^c 喜马望山(Himavant):人格化的喜马拉雅山脉,即印度教中的雪山神,是恒河女神之父。参照前注。

托马斯·斯特恩斯·艾略特 Thomas Stearns Eliot

哒亚德万：我听见那钥匙[46]
在门上转动了一次，只一次
我们想到钥匙，各自在牢房
每人想到钥匙，各自确认牢房
415　只有在黄昏，缥缈的传说才能
让垮掉的科里奥兰纳斯复活片刻[a]
哒
哒密阿塔：船儿愉快地回应
那撑帆划桨的行家里手
420　大海平静，你的心，受到邀请，
也会愉快地回应，随着自制之手
顺从地跳动[b]

　　　　　我坐在岸上
垂钓，背后是一片干燥的原野[47]
425　我是否至少该把自己的家园整理好？[c]

伦敦桥要垮掉了垮掉了垮掉了[d]
他随即隐没在那炼化之火中[48]
何时我才能像燕子一般——哦，燕子，燕子[49]

---

[a] 科里奥兰纳斯（Coriolanus）：莎士比亚以其名为题所作历史悲剧的人物，公元前5世纪罗马大将，出于狂傲，两次背叛而败亡。这里借他之名描写人陷于自己的精神牢房，只有在夜间借助天启忘掉自我，才能复活片刻。
[b] 指内心的自制会令生命历程一帆风顺。
[c] 典出《圣经·以赛亚书》第38章第1节："耶和华这样说，你要把你的家整顿妥当，因为你快要死去，不能存活。"
[d] 着名儿歌《伦敦桥要垮掉了》里还有一句"拿一把钥匙锁起她"。

托马斯·斯特恩斯·艾略特 Thomas Stearns Eliot

    那阿基坦王子在毁弃的塔楼中[50]
430 我用了这些散片支撑我的废墟
    好吧,我就遵你所嘱。希罗尼莫又疯了。[51]
    哒塔。哒亚德万。哒密阿塔。

        玄静   玄静   玄静[52]

作者原注

[1] 这首诗,不仅标题,甚至构思以及随之而来的大部分象征手法,都来自杰西·L.韦斯顿小姐有关圣杯传说的着作《从祭仪到传奇》(麦克米兰版)一书的启发。我从其中借鉴之多,可以说韦斯顿小姐的着作远比我自己的注释更能解答诗中的疑难之处;因而无论谁认为值得寻求解答,我都向他推荐这本书(且不说此书本身就引人入胜)。总的来说我还受益于深深影响了我们这一代人的另一部人类学着作;我指的是《金枝》;而主要用到的是《阿多尼斯、阿提斯、奥西里斯》两卷。熟悉这两部着作的人都会立即认出诗中提及的一些有关繁衍生长的仪式。

一、葬亡

[2] 第20行。参阅《以西结书》第二章第一节。
【译者按】艾略特指的是《圣经·旧约·以西结书》中"他对我说:人子啊,你站起来,我要和你说话。"】
[3] 23。参阅《传道书》第十二章第五节。
【译者按】诗人指的是《圣经·旧约·传道书》中警示老年凄

托马斯·斯特恩斯·艾略特 Thomas Stearns Eliot

惶的一段:"人怕高处,路上有惊慌;杏树开花,蚱蜢成为重担,欲望不再挑起;因为人归他永远的家,吊丧的在街上往来。"】

⁴ 31。见《特里斯坦与伊索尔德》第一幕第 5—8 行。
【译者按】德国音乐家瓦格纳歌剧《特里斯坦与伊索尔德》描写特里斯坦骑士与伊索尔德的爱情悲剧。伊索尔德被用船带到康沃尔与特里斯坦的叔叔马克王成婚,这是她在船上听到一名水手思念女友时唱的歌。】

⁵ 42。同上,第三幕第 24 行。
【译者按】原文是濒死的特里斯坦在等待伊索尔德时,帮他瞭望大海的牧羊人告诉他的话。】

⁶ 46。我并不熟悉塔罗纸牌的确切构成,我与之有所偏离显然是出于为我所用的目的。这套纸牌传统构成中那张倒悬者之所以合我所用是由于以下两点:我在心里把他同弗雷泽【译者按】即上述《金枝》的作者)的倒悬的神相联系,也同第五节中去以马忤斯的罩着头的使徒相联系。腓尼基水手和商人稍后出现;而"成群的人"和"溺亡"放在第四节处理。至于"持三根权杖的人"(塔罗牌中实有的一张),我则自作主张地把他跟渔王联系在一起。

⁷ 60。参见波德莱尔:

"人群涌动的城,充满迷梦的城,
那里幽灵在光天化日下搭讪过路的人。"

【译者按】原文出自波德莱尔诗集《恶之花》中的一首诗《七个老头子》(*Les Sept Viellards*)。中文为译者提供。】

⁸ 63。参见《地狱篇》第三章第 55—57 行:

托马斯·斯特恩斯·艾略特 Thomas Stearns Eliot

"一大群人
排成长龙,我简直不敢相信,
死神竟毁掉这么多人的生命。"

【译者按】《神曲·地狱篇》中但丁在冥间见到一大群人在巨痛中呻吟时发出的惊叹。本书所引但丁《神曲》中文皆摘自黄文捷译本。】

[9] 64。参看《神曲·地狱篇》第四章第25-27行:
"这里,从送入耳际的声音来看,
没有别的,只有长吁短叹,
这叹声使流动在这永劫之地的空气也不住抖颤。"

[10] 68。这是我时常注意到的情景。

[11] 74。参看韦伯斯特《白魔》中的挽歌。
【译者按】艾略特指的是第五幕第四场中"哦,把那狼弄远点,那是人类的敌人"。诗中"the Dog"则指天狼星/犬星Sirius。】

[12] 76。见波德莱尔《恶之花》前言。

二、棋局

[13] 77。参见《安东尼与克莉奥佩特拉》第二幕第二场第190行。
【译者按】艾略特指莎士比亚该剧中的描述:"她乘坐的画舫,像锃亮的御座/闪耀在水面上"。】

[14] 92。镶板顶棚。见维吉尔《埃涅阿斯纪》第一部第726行:
燃烧的灯挂在镶板顶棚上,
火把的烈焰驱走了黑夜。

【译者按】转译自 T.C. William 的英译:"from the gilded vault/far-blazing cressets swing, or torches bright/drive the dark

托马斯・斯特恩斯・艾略特 Thomas Stearns Eliot

night away",描写的是迦太基女王狄多举办盛宴招待埃涅阿斯的场景。狄多爱上埃涅阿斯,后为爱而死。】

15 98。田野风光。见弥尔顿《失乐园》第四卷第 140 行。
【译者按】艾略特指的是撒旦进入伊甸园时看到的田野风光,之后他诱惑了夏娃及亚当,致他们被贬入苦难世界,难免一死。】

16 99。见奥维德《变形记》第六卷菲洛墨拉。
【译者按】希腊神话,菲洛墨拉是雅典公主,被姐夫色雷斯国王忒鲁斯强奸后悲愤而变成夜莺。】

17 100。见本诗第三节第 204 行。

18 115。见本诗第三节第 195 行。

19 118。参见韦伯斯特:"风还在门边吹么?"
【译者按】指韦伯斯特戏剧《魔鬼的诉讼案》(*The Devil's Law Case*) 第三幕第二场中一位外科医生的问话。】

20 126。见本诗第一节第 37 和 48 行。

21 138。参见米德尔顿剧《女人谨防女人》中的棋局。
【译者按】指托马斯・米德尔顿(Thomas Middleton)在 *Women beware Women* 剧中所描述的棋局,局中每一招棋都与另一间屋子里佛罗伦萨公爵实施诱奸的步骤相对应。】

三、火诫

22 176。参看斯宾塞《婚礼歌》。
【译者按】指其中每一段结尾处的叠句,试译如下:"在此新婚之日,这短暂一刻:/可爱的泰晤士河啊,你轻轻地流,等我唱完我的歌。"诗人在此反其意而化用之。】

23 192。参见《暴风雨》第一幕第二场。
【译者按】指莎士比亚剧中斐迪南的台词,试译如下:"当

托马斯·斯特恩斯·艾略特 Thomas Stearns Eliot

我坐在岸上,再次哭悼我那父王的海难,这音乐贴着水面掠过我身边。"】

²⁴ 196。参见安德鲁·马维尔《致他的忸怩女友》。
【译者按】艾略特指的是 To His Coy Mistress 中诗句"可是在我背后总能听见/时间战车插翅逼近眼前。"见附录所载译者译文。】

²⁵ 197。参见约翰·戴《蜜蜂议会》:

"只要侧耳聆听,你会忽然听见
喇叭和打猎的声响,春天这声响
会把阿克泰恩送到戴安娜的身旁,
在那大家都能看到她赤裸的肌肤……"【译者自译】

²⁶ 199。这几行词摘自一首民谣,我并不知道这首民谣的出处:我是在澳大利亚悉尼间接听来的。

²⁷ 202。见魏尔伦着《帕西法尔》。
【译者按】《帕西法尔》中有句: "Et O ces voix d'enfants, chantant dans la coupole!"】

²⁸ 210。葡萄干报价为"伦敦到岸价免运费保险费";提单等文件在收到即期汇票时交付买方。

²⁹ 218。提瑞舍斯虽然只是个旁观者而算不上"人物",却是这首诗中最重要的角色,他串起了所有其他人物。就像独眼商人和葡萄干推销者可以融合为腓尼基水手,而后者与那不勒斯王子斐迪南也不能完全分开一样,所有的女人也都是同一个女人,而男女两种性别则在提瑞舍斯身上合为一体。提瑞舍斯所"见到"的,其实正是诗的实质内容。奥维德写的整个这一段富有人类学意义:

……他们说,朱庇特很快乐
(酒后)感觉很兴奋,忘掉了

托马斯・斯特恩斯・艾略特 Thomas Stearns Eliot

拘束和谨慎,于是消磨着时间
和朱诺开玩笑。"我认为,"他对她说
"你们女人从做爱中能得到更多快乐
比起我们可怜的男人。"她不同意,
所以两人决定把这个问题交给
见多识广的提瑞舍斯评判:他了解
做爱时男女两方面的感觉。
有一次他遇到了两条蛇在交配
在绿色的树林里,就把它们打散了,
于是,他从男人变成了女人,
做了七年女人后,又一次看到
这两条蛇交配,又一次把它们打
散了,一边说:"如果有这样的魔法
给你一击,男人就能变成女人,
或许女人也能变成男人。值得一试。"
于是他又变成了男人;作为裁判,
他站在朱庇特一边。而朱诺
是个输不起的人,她说裁判
总是闭着眼,就把他变成永远如此。
一个神不能推翻另一个神的行为,
但全能的天父出于怜悯,
作为补偿,赋予了提瑞舍斯
预知未来的能力,获得一些
荣耀以减轻他所受的惩罚。

【译者按】这段诗系译者根据罗尔夫•汉弗莱斯(Rolphe Humphries)英译奥维德《变形记:提瑞舍斯的故事》第三卷第 318-343 行转译。】

托马斯·斯特恩斯·艾略特 Thomas Stearns Eliot

30 221。这一行与萨福的原诗句也许并不完全一样，不过我想的是"海边"或"小渔船"渔夫傍晚回家的情景。

31 253。参照哥尔德史密斯（Goldsmith）《威克菲尔德的牧师》中的歌。
【译者按】指第二十四章中奥莉维亚回到自己被诱奸之地时所唱的歌，见本书所列译文。】

32 257。见《暴风雨》，同上。
【译者按】指原注192行。】

33 264。我认为马格纳斯殉道堂的室内设计是雷恩最精美的室内建筑作品之一。见《建议拆除的十九座市内教堂》(P. S. King & Son, Ltd.)。

34 266。泰晤士河（3位）女儿的歌开始于此。从292行到306行她们轮流发话。参见《诸神的黄昏》第三幕第一场：莱茵河女儿。

35 279。见弗劳德着《伊丽莎白》第一卷第四章，德夸德拉致西班牙国王菲利普的信：

> "下午我们乘着画舫在河上观看赛事。她（女王）单独与罗伯特伯爵还有我自己在船尾甲板上，这时他们说话开始不着边际起来，甚至到头来罗伯特伯爵还说，既然我就在场，只要女王乐意，他们俩当即成婚也无不可。"

【译者按】詹姆士·安东尼·弗劳德是英国历史学家；阿尔瓦雷斯·德夸德拉是西班牙一位主教兼驻英大使。罗伯特即罗伯特·达德利，第一代莱斯特伯爵，英国女王伊丽莎白一世的宠臣。传闻二人一向亲密，但也可能只是政治同谋而已。】

36 293。参阅《炼狱篇》第五首第133行：

托马斯·斯特恩斯·艾略特 Thomas Stearns Eliot

> "请记住我,我就是那个皮娅,
> 锡耶纳养育了我,而马雷马却把我毁掉。"

【译者按】这些是《神曲·炼狱篇》中锡耶纳的托洛梅伊在炼狱遇到但丁时说的话,讲述她生在锡耶纳,又在马雷马被丈夫所谋杀之事。】

37 307。见圣奥古斯丁的《忏悔录》:

> "于是我来到了迦太基,这里形形色色
> 骚动的邪爱唱响在我耳旁。"

38 308。这些词语引自佛陀的火戒(其重要性相当于耶稣的山上宝训)。全文可见已故亨利·克拉克·沃伦的《佛教英译》(*Buddhism in Translation*)(哈佛东方丛书)。沃伦先生是西方佛学研究的伟大先驱之一。

【译者按】赵萝蕤先生在其译者按中所译的火戒这一段非常优美,可供参考,此不另译。大意是一切感官,一切欲望都在燃烧,信众应善加克服,以期解脱。】

39 309。仍见于圣奥古斯丁的《忏悔录》。苦修主义在东方与西方的这两个代表能并列一处,成为本诗这一部分的完结,并非偶然。

五、雷之语

40 第五节第一部分有三个主题:去往以马忤斯、走近凶险教堂(见韦斯顿小姐的著作)、东欧今日的衰微。

41 357。这是我在魁北克省听到过的隐夜鸫(Turdus aonalaschkae pallasii)。查普曼说(《北美东部鸟类手册》)"这种鸟最喜僻静的林木丛……它的叫声不很多样,音量也不大,而其声调的纯净甜美和精致婉转则是无与伦比的。"它那"滴水歌声"名不虚传。

托马斯・斯特恩斯・艾略特 Thomas Stearns Eliot

[42] 360。下面这几行是受到一篇南极探险纪行（我忘记是哪篇了，可能是沙克尔顿（Shackleton）的那篇）激发所得。据说探险队员们精疲力竭之时，一直有个错觉，好像比清点到的人数还多出一人。

[43] 366-376。参见赫尔曼・黑塞《混沌一瞥》：

> "半个欧洲，至少半个东欧，已经在走向混乱，怀着神圣的妄想醉醺醺地沿着深渊挪动，同时也在歌唱，像德米特里・卡拉马索夫（Dmitri Karamasoff）那样醉醺醺地唱着颂歌。受到冒犯的布尔乔亚听到发出嘲笑，圣人和先知听到则泪流不已。"

[44] 401。"Datta, dayadhvam, dāmyata"（施舍、仁慈、自制）。关于雷声意义的寓言见于《大森林奥义书》（*Brihadaranyaka--Upanishad*）第五卷第一章。译文见保罗・雅各布・德森（Deussen）的《吠陀的六十篇奥义书》（*Sechzig Upanishads des Veda*）第489页。

【译者按】《大森林奥义书》中的这一段，此处借用黄宝生先生的中文译本如下：

> 生主的三支后裔天神、凡人和阿修罗曾经作为梵行者，住在父亲生主那里。梵行期满后，天神们说道："请您给我们指示。"于是，生主对他们说了一个音节："Da。"然后，问道："你们理解吗？"他们回答说："我们理解。您对我们说：'你们要自制（dāmyata）！'生主说道："唵，你们已经理解。"
>
> 注："梵行者"指学生。按照婆罗门教，人生的第一阶段是梵行期，即拜师求学。
>
> 然后，凡人们对生主说道："请您给我们指示。"生主对他们说了一个音节："Da。"然后，问道：

托马斯·斯特恩斯·艾略特 Thomas Stearns Eliot

"你们理解吗？"他们回答说："我们理解。您对我们说：'你们要施舍（datta）！'"生主说道："唵，你们已经理解。"

然后，阿修罗们对生主说道："请您给我们指示。"生主对他们说了一个音节："Da。"然后，问道："你们理解吗？"他们回答说："我们理解。您对我们说：'你们要仁慈（dayadhvam）！'"生主说道："唵，你们已经理解。"

作为天国之声的雷鸣回响着："Da，Da，Da！"也就是"你们要自制！你们要施舍！你们要仁慈！因此，应该学会这三者：自制、施舍和仁慈。〕

[45] 407。参见韦伯斯特《白魔》第五幕第六场：

"她们又将改嫁
不等蛆虫蛀穿你的裹尸布，不等蜘蛛
为你的墓志铭织起薄幕。"

[46] 411。参见《炼狱篇》第三十三首第46行：

"我听到可怕塔楼的下层，
传来钉门的声音。"

又见 F.H.布拉德雷《表象与实在》第346页：

"我的外在感觉跟我的思想感情一样，都是只属于我个人的。在这两方面，我的经历都落在我个人的圈子内，对外是封闭的；每一个领域中的所有因素都一样，都与周围的领域相隔绝。简而言之，整个世界，如果看作是显现给某灵魂的存在，它对那个灵魂就是独特的、私密的。"

【译者按】《神曲·炼狱篇》中的引文是乌格里诺（Ugolino della Gherardesca）回忆起他同他的两个儿子两个孙子被锁在塔楼

托马斯·斯特恩斯·艾略特 Thomas Stearns Eliot

中,活活饿死时所说。他听到钥匙只转一圈是因为狱吏锁门后就将钥匙扔进河里。他是因为背叛(科里奥兰纳斯也背着背叛之名)而被囚。另外,艾略特在哈佛大学的博士论文题为《F.H.布拉德利的哲学中的知识与经验》。】

47 424。见韦斯顿《从祭仪到传奇》中有关渔王的一章。
【译者按】韦斯顿在有关渔王的一章讨论了作为普世生命象征的鱼,有着古老的历史。它与创造生命保护生命的神相通。】

48 427。见《炼狱篇》第二十六首第 148 行:

"'我现在请求您,看在那神力的份上
——它正在引导您走向那山梯的顶峰,
您能及时记得我的悲痛!'
他随即隐没在那冶炼他的烈火之中。"

49 428。见《维纳斯的守夜》。参照第二、三节中的菲洛墨拉。
【译者按】"何时我才能像燕子一般"原文为拉丁文:"Quando fiam uti chelidon",来自佚名作品《维纳斯的守夜》(*Pervigilium Veneris*),作品中有句"她在唱,而我哑然。我的春天何时来?/何时我才能像燕子一般,不再无声?"
"哦,燕子,燕子"应是出自丁尼生的长篇叙事诗《公主》,其中有句:"哦,燕子,燕子,飞啊,向南飞。"】

50 429。见热拉尔·德·内瓦尔的十四行诗《苦难的人》。
【译者按】热拉尔·德·内瓦尔(Gerard de Nerval)是法国诗人热拉尔·拉布吕尼(Gérard Labrunie)的笔名。其代表作十四行诗《苦难的人》(*El Desdichado*)开篇,试译如下:

我就是那阴暗者,——那鳏居者,——那悲极之人,
那阿基坦王子在毁弃的塔楼上:
我的孤星已死,——而我那缀星的琴
承载着忧伤郁结的黑色太阳。

托马斯·斯特恩斯·艾略特 Thomas Stearns Eliot

原文为法文：

> Je suis le Ténébreux, - le Veuf, - l'Inconsolé,
> Le Prince d'Aquitaine à la Tour abolie:
> Ma seule Etoile est morte, - et mon luth constellé
> Porte le Soleil noir de la Mélancolie.】

51　431。见基德《西班牙悲剧》。

【译者按】即托马斯·基德（Thomas Kyd）所著 *Spanish Tragedy*。基德该剧是后来莎士比亚悲剧《哈姆雷特》的早期先导之一。希罗尼莫由于儿子霍拉肖遭嫉被害而发疯。意欲复仇，正不知所措，却被仇人邀请写一部剧以为宫廷娱乐。他便答应了，说"Why then *Ile fit you*"（古英文"我就遵你所嘱"），于是把儿子被害的故事和人物写进剧中，并请仇人参演剧中角色，趁机杀死谋害儿子的凶手。希罗尼莫的剧中剧也是悲剧，他写的剧中关键人物也都要死掉。希罗尼莫该剧以多种语言结尾，艾略特此诗承袭了这一手法。】

52　433。玄静（Shantih），如此重复，为《奥义书》的正规结语。"超越人所能理解的平安"略可译之。

【译者按】艾略特所引之句来自《圣经·新约·腓立比书》第四章第七节："神所赐那超越人所能了解的平安，必在基督耶稣里，保守你们的心怀意念。"】

The Waste Land

"Nam Sibyllam quidem Cumis ego ipse oculis meis vidi in ampulla pendere, et cum illi pueri dicerent: Σιβνλλατιθελειζ; repondebat illa: αποθαν ειν θελω."

For Ezra Pound
il miglior fabbro.

I. The Burial of the Dead

April is the cruellest month, breeding
Lilacs out of the dead land, mixing
Memory and desire, stirring
Dull roots with spring rain.
Winter kept us warm, covering
Earth in forgetful snow, feeding
A little life with dried tubers.
Summer surprised us, coming over the Starnbergersee
With a shower of rain; we stopped in the colonnade,
And went on in sunlight, into the Hofgarten,
And drank coffee, and talked for an hour.
Bin gar keine Russin, stamm' aus Litauen, echt deutsch.
And when we were children, staying at the archduke's,
My cousin's, he took me out on a sled,
And I was frightened. He said, Marie,

托马斯·斯特恩斯·艾略特 Thomas Stearns Eliot

Marie, hold on tight. And down we went.
In the mountains, there you feel free.
I read, much of the night, and go south in the winter.

What are the roots that clutch, what branches grow
Out of this stony rubbish? Son of man,
You cannot say, or guess, for you know only
A heap of broken images, where the sun beats,
And the dead tree gives no shelter, the cricket no relief,
And the dry stone no sound of water. Only
There is shadow under this red rock,
(Come in under the shadow of this red rock),
And I will show you something different from either
Your shadow at morning striding behind you
Or your shadow at evening rising to meet you;
I will show you fear in a handful of dust.

  Frish weht der Wind
  Der Heimat zu
  Mein Irisch Kind,
  Wo weilest du?

"You gave me hyacinths first a year ago;
They called me the hyacinth girl."
--Yet when we came back, late, from the Hyacinth garden,
Your arms full, and your hair wet, I could not
Speak, and my eyes failed, I was neither
Living nor dead, and I knew nothing,

托马斯·斯特恩斯·艾略特 Thomas Stearns Eliot

Looking into the heart of light, the silence.
Oed' und leer das Meer.

Madame Sosostris, famous clairvoyante,
Had a bad cold, nevertheless
Is known to be the wisest woman in Europe,
With a wicked pack of cards. Here, said she,
Is your card, the drowned Phoenician Sailor,
(Those are pearls that were his eyes. Look!)
Here is Belladonna, the Lady of the Rocks,
The lady of situations.
Here is the man with three staves, and here the Wheel,
And here is the one-eyed merchant, and this card,
Which is blank, is something he carries on his back,
Which I am forbidden to see. I do not find
The Hanged Man. Fear death by water.
I see crowds of people, walking round in a ring,
Thank you. If you see dear Mrs. Equitone,
Tell her I bring the horoscope myself:
One must be so careful these days.

Unreal City,
Under the brown fog of a winter dawn,
A crowd flowed over London Bridge, so many,
I had not thought death had undone so many.
Sighs, short and infrequent, were exhaled,
And each man fixed his eyes before his feet.
Flowed up the hill and down King William Street,

托马斯·斯特恩斯·艾略特 Thomas Stearns Eliot

To where Saint Mary Woolnoth kept the hours
With a dead sound on the final stroke of nine.
There I saw one I knew, and stopped him, crying: "Stetson!
"You who were with me in the ships at Mylae!
"That corpse you planted last year in your garden,
"Has it begun to sprout? Will it bloom this year?
"Or has the sudden frost disturbed its bed?
"O keep the Dog far hence, that's friend to men,
"Or with his nails he'll dig it up again!
"You! *Hypocrite lecteur!---mon semblable,--mon frere!*"

II. A Game of Chess

The Chair she sat in, like a burnished throne,
Glowed on the marble, where the glass
Held up by standards wrought with fruited vines
From which a golden Cupidon peeped out
(Another hid his eyes behind his wing)
Doubled the flames of sevenbranched candelabra
Reflecting light upon the table as
The glitter of her jewels rose to meet it,
From satin cases poured in rich profusion.
In vials of ivory and colored glass
Unstoppered, lurked her strange synthetic perfumes,
Unguent, powdered, or liquid--troubled, confused
And drowned the sense in odors; stirred by the air
That freshened from the window, these ascended
In flattening the prolonged candle flames,

托马斯·斯特恩斯·艾略特 Thomas Stearns Eliot

Flung their smoke into the laquearia,
Stirring the pattern on the coffered ceiling.
Huge sea-wood fed with copper
Burned green and orange, framed by the colored stone,
In which sad light a carved dolphin swam.
Above the antique mantel was displayed
As though a window gave upon the sylvan scene
The change of Philomel, by the barbarous king
So rudely forced; yet there the nightingale
Filled all the desert with inviolable voice
And still she cried, and still the world pursues,
"Jug Jug" to dirty ears.
And other withered stumps of time
Were told upon the walls; staring forms
Leaned out, leaning, hushing the room enclosed.
Footsteps shuffled on the stair.
Under the firelight, under the brush, her hair
Spread out in fiery points
Glowed into words, then would be savagely still.

"My nerves are bad tonight. Yes, bad. Stay with me.
"Speak to me. Why do you never speak. Speak.
"What are you thinking of? What thinking? What?
"I never know what you are thinking. Think."

I think we are in rats' alley
Where the dead men lost their bones.

托马斯·斯特恩斯·艾略特 Thomas Stearns Eliot

"What is that noise?"
  The wind under the door.
"What is that noise now? What is the wind doing?"
    Nothing again nothing.
      "Do
"You know nothing? Do you see nothing? Do you remember
"Nothing?"

  I remember
Those are pearls that were his eyes.
"Are you alive, or not? Is there nothing in your head?"
 But
O O O O that Shakespeherian Rag---
It's so elegant
So intelligent
  "What shall I do now? What shall I do?"
"I shall rush out as I am, and walk the street
"With my hair down, so. What shall we do tomorrow?
"What shall we ever do?"
    The hot water at ten.
And if it rains, a closed car at four.
And we shall play a game of chess,
Pressing lidless eyes and waiting for a knock upon the door.

When Lil's husband got demobbed, I said--
I didn't mince my words, I said to her myself,
HURRY UP PLEASE IT'S TIME
Now Albert's coming back, make yourself a bit smart.

托马斯·斯特恩斯·艾略特 Thomas Stearns Eliot

He'll want to know what you done with that money he gave you
To get yourself some teeth. He did, I was there.
You have them all out, Lil, and get a nice set,
He said, I swear, I can't bear to look at you.
And no more can't I, I said, and think of poor Albert,
He's been in the army four years, he wants a good time,
And if you don't give it him, there's others will, I said.
Oh is there, she said. Something o' that, I said.
Then I'll know who to thank, she said, and give me a straight look.
HURRY UP PLEASE ITS TIME
If you don't like it you can get on with it, I said.
Others can pick and choose if you can't.
But if Albert makes off, it won't be for lack of telling.
You ought to be ashamed, I said, to look so antique.
(And her only thirty-one.)
I can't help it, she said, pulling a long face,
It's them pills I took, to bring it off, she said.
(She's had five already, and nearly died of young George.)
The chemist said it would be all right, but I've never been the same.
You are a proper fool, I said.
Well, if Albert won't leave you alone, there it is, I said,
What you get married for if you don't want children?
HURRY UP PLEASE ITS TIME
Well, that Sunday Albert was home, they had a hot gammon,
And they asked me in to dinner, to get the beauty of it hot--
HURRY UP PLEASE ITS TIME

托马斯·斯特恩斯·艾略特 Thomas Stearns Eliot

HURRY UP PLEASE ITS TIME
Goonight Bill. Goonight Lou. Goonight May. Goonight.
Ta ta. Goonight. Goonight.
Good night, ladies, good night, sweet ladies, good night, good night.

III. The Fire Sermon

The river's tent is broken: the last fingers of leaf
Clutch and sink into the wet bank. The wind
Crosses the brown land, unheard. The nymphs are departed.
Sweet Thames, run softly, till I end my song.
The river bears no empty bottles, sandwich papers,
Silk handkerchiefs, cardboard boxes, cigarette ends
Or other testimony of summer nights. The nymphs are departed.
And their friends, the loitering heirs of City directors;
Departed, have left no addresses.
By the waters of Leman I Sat down and wept...
Sweet Thames, run softly till I end my song,
Sweet Thames, run softly, for I speak not loud or long.
But at my back in a cold blast I hear
The rattle of the bones, and chuckle spread from ear to ear.

A rat crept softly through the vegetation
Dragging its slimy belly on the bank
While I was fishing in the dull canal
On a winter evening round behind the gashouse
Musing upon the king my brother's wreck

托马斯·斯特恩斯·艾略特 Thomas Stearns Eliot

And on the king my father's death before him.
White bodies naked on the low damp ground
And bones cast in a little low dry garret,
Rattled by the rat's foot only, year to year.
But at my back from time to time I hear
The sound of horns and motors, which shall bring
Sweeney to Mrs. Porter in the spring.
O the moon shone bright on Mrs. Porter
And on her daughter
They wash their feet in soda water
Et O ces voix d'enfants, chantant dans la coupole!

Twit twit twit
Jug jug jug jug jug jug
So rudely forc'd.
Terue

Unreal City
Under the brown fog of a winter noon
Mr. Eugenides, the Smyrna merchant
Unshaven, with a pocket full of currants
C.i.f. London: documents at sight,
Asked me in demotic French
To luncheon at the Cannon Street Hotel
Followed by a weekend at the Metropole.

At the violet hour, when the eyes and back
Turn upward from the desk, when the human engine waits

托马斯·斯特恩斯·艾略特 Thomas Stearns Eliot

Like a taxi throbbing waiting,
I Tiresias, though blind, throbbing between two lives,
Old man with wrinkled female breasts, can see
At the violet hour, the evening hour that strives
Homeward, and brings the sailor home from sea,
The typist home at teatime, clears her breakfast, lights
Her stove, and lays out food in tins.
Out of the window perilously spread
Her drying combinations touched by the sun's last rays,
On the divan are piled (at night by her bed)
Stockings, slippers, camisoles, and stays.
I Tiresias, old man with wrinkled dugs
Perceived the scene, and foretold the rest--
I too awaited the expected guest.
He, the young man carbuncular, arrives,
A small house agent's clerk, with one bold stare,
One of the low on whom assurance sits
As a silk hat on a Bradford millionaire.
The time is now propitious, as he guesses,
The meal is ended, she is bored and tired,
Endeavors to engage her in caresses
Which still are unreproved, if undesired.
Flushed and decided, he assaults at once;
Exploring hands encounter no defense;
His vanity requires no response,
And makes a welcome of indifference.
(And I Tiresias have foresuffered all
Enacted on this same divan or bed;

托马斯·斯特恩斯·艾略特 Thomas Stearns Eliot

I who have sat by Thebes below the wall
And walked among the lowest of the dead.)
Bestows one final patronizing kiss,
And gropes his way, finding the stairs unlit...

She turns and looks a moment in the glass,
Hardly aware of her departed lover;
Her brain allows one half-formed thought to pass:
"Well now that's done: and I'm glad it's over."
When lovely woman stoops to folly and
Paces about her room again, alone,
She smoothes her hair with automatic hand,
And puts a record on the gramophone.

"This music crept by me upon the waters"
And along the Strand, up Queen Victoria Street.
O City city, I can sometimes hear
Beside a public bar in Lower Thames Street,
The pleasant whining of a mandolin
And a clatter and a chatter from within
Where fishmen lounge at noon: where the walls
Of Magnus Martyr I hold
Inexplicable splendor of Ionian white and gold.

    The river sweats
    Oil and tar
    The barges drift
    With the turning tide

托马斯·斯特恩斯·艾略特 Thomas Stearns Eliot

Red sails
Wide
To leeward, swing on the heavy spar.
The barges wash
Drifting logs
Down Greenwich reach
Past the Isle of Dogs.
     Weialala leia
     Wallala leialala

Elizabeth and Leicester
Beating oars
The stern was formed
A gilded shell
Red and gold
The brisk swell
Rippled both shores
Southwest wind
Carried down stream
The peal of bells
White towers
     Weialala leia
     Wallala leialala

"Trams and dusty trees.
Highbury bore me. Richmond and Kew
Undid me. By Richmond I raised my knees
Supine on the floor of a narrow canoe."

托马斯·斯特恩斯·艾略特 Thomas Stearns Eliot

"My feet are at Moorgate, and my heart
Under my feet. After the event
He wept. He promised a new start.'
I made no comment. What should I resent?"

"On Margate Sands.
I can connect
Nothing with Nothing.
The broken fingernails of dirty hands.
My people humble people who expect
Nothing."
la la

To Carthage then I came

Burning burning burning burning
O Lord Thou pluckest me out
O Lord Thou pluckest

burning

IV. Death by Water

Phlebas the Phoenician, a fortnight dead,
Forgot the cry of gulls, and the deep sea swell
And the profit and loss.
    A current under sea
Picked his bones in whispers. As he rose and fell

托马斯·斯特恩斯·艾略特 Thomas Stearns Eliot

He passed the stages of his age and youth
Entering the whirlpool.
                    Gentle or Jew
O you who turn the wheel and look to windward,
Consider Phlebas, who was once handsome and tall as you.

V. What the Thunder Said

After the torchlight red on sweaty faces
After the frosty silence in the gardens
After the agony in stony places
The shouting and the crying
Prison and palace and reverberation
Of thunder of spring over distant mountains
He who was living is now dead
We who were living are now dying
With a little patience

Here is no water but only rock
Rock and no water and the sandy road
The road winding above among the mountains
Which are mountains of rock without water
If there were water we should stop and drink
Amongst the rock one cannot stop or think
Sweat is dry and feet are in the sand
If there were only water amongst the rock
Dead mountain mouth of carious teeth that cannot spit
Here one can neither stand nor lie nor sit

托马斯·斯特恩斯·艾略特 Thomas Stearns Eliot

There is not even silence in the mountains
But dry sterile thunder without rain
There is not even solitude in the mountains
But red sullen faces sneer and snarl
From doors of mudcracked houses
                If there were water
    And no rock
    If there were rock
    And also water
    And water
    A spring
    A pool among the rock
    If there were the sound of water only
    Not the cicada
    And dry grass singing
    But sound of water over a rock
    Where the hermit thrush sings in the pine trees
    Drip drop drip drop drop drop drop
    But there is no water

Who is the third who walks always beside you?
When I count, there are only you and I together
But when I look ahead up the white road
There is always another one walking beside you
Gliding wrapped in a brown mantle, hooded
I do not know whether a man of a woman
---But who is that on the other side of you?

托马斯·斯特恩斯·艾略特 Thomas Stearns Eliot

What is that sound high in the air
Murmur of maternal lamentation
Who are those hooded hordes swarming
Over endless plains, stumbling in cracked earth
Ringed by the flat horizon only
What is the city over the mountains
Cracks and reforms and bursts in the violet air
Falling towers
Jerusalem Athens Alexandria
Vienna London
Unreal

A woman drew her long black hair out tight
And fiddled whisper music on those strings
And bats with baby faces in the violet light
Whistled, and beat their wings
And crawled head downward down a blackened wall
And upside down in air were towers
Tolling reminiscent bells, that kept the hours
And voices singing out of empty cisterns and exhausted wells.

In this decayed hole among the mountains
In the faint moonlight, the grass is singing
Over the tumbled graves, about the chapel
There is the empty chapel, only the wind's home.
It has no windows, and the door swings,
Dry bones can harm no one.
Only a cock stood on the rooftree

托马斯·斯特恩斯·艾略特 Thomas Stearns Eliot

Co co rico co co rico
In a flash of lightning. Then a damp gust
Bringing rain

Ganga was sunken, and the limp leaves
Waited for rain, while the black clouds
Gathered far distant, over Himavant.
The jungle crouched, humped in silence.
Then spoke the thunder
Da
Datta: what have we given?
My friend, blood shaking my heart
The awful daring of a moment's surrender
Which an age of prudence can never retract
By this, and this only, we have existed
Which is not to be found in our obituaries
Or in memories draped by the beneficent spider
Or under seals broken by the lean solicitor
In our empty rooms
Da
Dayadhvam: I have heard the key
Turn in the door once and turn once only
We think of the key, each in his prison
Thinking of the key, each confirms a prison
Only at nightfall, ethereal rumors
Revive for a moment a broken Coriolanus
Da
Damyata: The boat responded

托马斯·斯特恩斯·艾略特 Thomas Stearns Eliot

Gaily, to the hand expert with sail and oar
The sea was calm, your heart would have responded
Gaily, when invited, beating obedient
To controlling hands

  I sat upon the shore
Fishing, with the arid plain behind me
Shall I at least set my lands in order?
London Bridge is falling down falling down falling down
Poi s'ascose nel foco che gli affina
Quando fiam uti chelidon---O swallow swallow
Le Prince d'Aquitainte a la tour abolie
These fragments I have shored against my ruins
Why then Ile fit you. Hieronymo's mad againe.
Datta. Dayadhvam. Damyata.

  Shantih shantih shantih

NOTES

Not only the title, but the plan and a good deal of the incidental symbolism of the poem were suggested by Miss Jessie L. Weston's book on the Grail legend: *From Ritual to Romance* (Cambridge). Indeed, so deeply am I indebted, Miss Weston's book will elucidate the difficulties of the poem much better than my notes can do; and I recommend it (apart from the great interest of the book itself) to any who think such elucidation of the poem worth the trouble. To another work of anthropology I am indebted in general, one which has influenced our generation profoundly; I mean *The Golden Bough*; I have used especially the two volumes *Adonis, Attis, Osiris*. Anyone who is acquainted with these works will immediately recognize in the poem certain references to vegetation ceremonies.

I. Burial of the Dead

20. Cf. Ezekiel II, i.
23. Cf. Ecclesiastes XII, v.
31. V. Tristan und Isolde, I, verses 5-8.
42. [V. Tristan und Isolde,] III, verse 24.
46. I am not familiar with the exact constitution of the Tarot pack of cards, from which I have obviously departed to suit my own convenience. The Hanged Man, a member of the traditional pack, fits my purpose in two ways: because he is associated in my mind with the Hanged God of Frazer, and because I associate him with the hooded figure in the passage of the disciples to Emmaus in Part V. The Phoenician Sailor and the Merchant appear later; also the "crowds of people," and Death by Water is executed in Part IV. The Man with Three Staves (an authentic member of the Tarot pack) I associate, quite arbitrarily, with the Fisher King himself.
60. Cf. Baudelaire

"Fourmillante cité, cité pleine de rêves,
"Où le spectre en plein jour raccroche le passant."
63. Cf. Inferno III, 55-57:

"si lunga tratta
di gente, ch'io non avrei mai creduto
che morte tanta n'avesse disfatta."
64. Cf. Inferno IV, 25-27:

托马斯·斯特恩斯·艾略特 Thomas Stearns Eliot

"Quivi, secondo che per ascoltare,
non avea pianto ma' che de sospiri,
che l'aura eterna facevan tremare."

68. A phenomenon which I have often noticed.

74. Cf. the Dirge in Webster's *White Devil*.

76. V. Baudelaire, Preface to *Fleurs du Mal*.

77. Cf. *Antony and Cleopatra*, II, ii, l. 190.

II. A Game of Chess

92. Laquearia. V. *Aeneid*, I, 726:

dependent lychni laquearibus incensi
aureis, et noctem flammis funalia vincunt

98. Sylvan scene. V. Milton, *Paradise Lost*, IV, 140.

99. V. Ovid, *Metamorphoses*, VI, Philomela.

100. Cf. Part III, l. 204.

115. Cf. Part III, l. 195.

118. Cf. Webster: "Is the wind in that door still?"

126. Cf. Part I, 37, 48.

138. Cf. The game of chess in Middleton's *Women Beware Women*.

III. The Fire Sermon

176. V. Spenser, *Prothalamion*.

192. Cf. *The Tempest*, I, ii.

196. Cf. Marvell, *To His Coy Mistress*.

197. Cf. Day, *Parliament of Bees*:

"When of the sudden, listening, you shall hear,
"A noise of horns and hunting, which shall bring

托马斯·斯特恩斯·艾略特 Thomas Stearns Eliot

"Actaeon to Diana in the spring,
"Where all shall see her naked skin…"

199. I do not know the origin of the ballad from which these lines are taken: it was reported to me from Sydney, Australia.

202. V. Verlaine, *Parsifal*.

210. The currants were quoted at a price "carriage and insurance free to London"; and the Bill of Lading etc. were to be handed to the buyer upon payment of the sight draft.

218. Tiresias, although a mere spectator and not indeed a "character," is yet the most important personage in the poem, uniting all the rest. Just as the one-eyed merchant, seller of currants, melts into the Phoenician Sailor, and the latter is not wholly distinct from Ferdinand Prince of Naples, so all the women are one woman, and the two sexes meet in Tiresias. What Tiresias *sees*, in fact, is the substance of the poem. The whole passage from Ovid is of great anthropological interest:

'…Cum Iunone iocos et maior vestra profecto est
Quam, quae contingit maribus,' dixisse, 'voluptas.'
Illa negat; placuit quae sit sententia docti
Quaerere Tiresiae: venus huic erat ultraque nota.
Nam duo magnorum viridi coeuntia silva
Corpora serpentum baculi violaverat ictu
Deque viro factus, mirabile, femina septem
Egerat autumnos; octavo rursus eosdem
Vidit et 'est vestrae si tanta potentia plagae,'
Dixit 'ut auctoris sortem in contraria mutet,
Nunc quoque vos feriam!' percussis anguibus isdem
Forma prior rediit genetivaque venit imago.
Arbiter hic igitur sumptus de lite iocosa
Dicta Iovis firmat; gravius Saturnia iusto
Nec pro materia fertur doluisse suique
Iudicis aeterna damnavit lumina nocte,

托马斯·斯特恩斯·艾略特 Thomas Stearns Eliot

>   At pater omnipotens (neque enim licet inrita cuiquam
>   Facta dei fecisse deo) pro lumine adempto
>   Scire futura dedit poenamque levavit honore.

221. This may not appear as exact as Sappho's lines, but I had in mind "longshore" or "dory" fisherman, who returns at nightfall.

253. V. Goldsmith, the song in *The Vicar of Wakefield*.

257. V. *The Tempest*, as above.

264. The interior of St. Magnus Martyr is to my mind one of the finest among Wren's interiors. See *The Proposed Demolition of Nineteen City Churches*: (P. S. King & Sons, Ltd.)

266. The Song of the (three) Thames-daughters begins here. From line 292 to 306 inclusive they speak in turn. V. *Götterdämmerung*, III, i: the Rhine-daughters.

279. V. Froude, *Elizabeth*, Vol. I, ch. iv, letter of De Quadra to Philip of Spain:

> "In the afternoon we were in a barge, watching the games on the river. (The queen) was alone with Lord Robert and myself on the poop, when they began to talk nonsense, and went so far that Lord Robert at last said, as I was on the spot there was no reason why they should not be married if the queen pleased."

293. Cf. *Purgatorio*, V, 133:

> "Ricorditi di me, che son la Pia;
> "Siena mi fe', disfecemi Maremma."

307. V. St. Augustine's *Confessions*: "to Carthage then I came, where a cauldron of unholy loves sang all about mine ears."

308. The complete text of the Buddha's Fire Sermon (which corresponds in importance to the Sermon on the Mount) from which these words are taken, will be found translated in the late Henry Clarke Warren's *Buddhism in Translation* (Harvard Oriental Series). Mr. Warren was one of the great pioneers of

Buddhist studies in the Occident.

309. From St. Augustine's *Confessions* again. The collocation of these two representatives of eastern and western ascetism, as the culmination of this part of the poem, is not an accident.

V. What the Thunder Said

In the first part of Part V three themes are employed: the journey to Emmaus, the approach to the Chapel Perilous (see Miss Weston's book) and the present decay of eastern Europe.

357. This is *Turdus aonalaschkae pallasii*, the hermit-thrush which I have heard in Quebec County. Chapman says (*Handbook of Birds of Eastern North America*) "it is most at home in secluded woodland and thickety retreats... Its notes are not remarkable for variety or volume, but in purity and sweetness of tone and exquisite modulation they are unequalled." Its "water-dripping song" is justly celebrated.

360. The following lines were stimulated by the account of one of the Antarctic expeditions (I forget which, but I think one of Shackleton's): it was related that the party of explorers, at the extremity of their strength, had the constant delusion that there was *one more member* than could actually be counted.

366-376. Cf. Hermann Hesse, *Blick ins chaos*:

> "Schon ist halb Europa, schon ist zumindest der halbe Osten Europas auf dem Wege zum Chaos, fährt betrunken im heiligem Wahn am Abgrund entlang und singt dazu, singt betrunken und hymnisch wie Dmitri Karamasoff sang. Ueber diese Lieder lacht der Bürger beleidigt, der Heilige und Seher hört sie mit Tränen."

401. "Datta, dayadhvam, damyata" (Give, sympathise, control). The fable of the meaning of the Thunder is found in the

托马斯·斯特恩斯·艾略特 Thomas Stearns Eliot

Brihadaranyaka—Upanishad, 5, 1. A translation is found in Deussen's Sechsig *Upanishads des Veda*, p. 489.

407. Cf. Webster, *The White Devil*, V, vi:

> "…they'll remarry
> Ere the worm pierce your winding-sheet, ere the spider
> Make a thin curtain for your epitaphs."

411. Cf. *Inferno*, XXXIII, 46:

> "ed io sentii chiavar l'uscio di sotto
> all'orribile torre."

Also F. H. Bradley, *Appearance and Reality*, p. 346:

> "My external sensations are no less private to myself than are my thoughts or my feelings. In either case my experience falls within my own circle, a circle closed on the outside; and, with all its elements alike, every sphere is opaque to the others which surround it… In brief, regarded as an existence which appears in a soul, the whole world for each is peculiar and private to that soul."

424. V. Weston: *From Ritual to Romance*; chapter on the Fisher King.

427. V. *Purgatorio*, XXVI, 148.

> "'Ara vos prec, per aquella valor
> 'que vos guida al som de l'escalina,
> 'sovegna vos a temps de ma dolor.'
> Poi s'ascose nel foco che gli affina."

428. V. *Pervigilium Veneris*. Cf. Philomela in Parts II and III.

429. V. Gerard de Nerval, Sonnet *El Desdichado*.

431. V. Kyd's *Spanish Tragedy*.

433. Shantih. Repeated as here, a formal ending to an Upanishad. "The Peace which passeth understanding" is a feeble translation of the content of the word.

J. 阿尔弗雷德·普鲁弗洛克的情歌

假如我相信我的话是回答
一个终究会返回世上的人,
这团火焰就会静止不摇曳了;
但是,既然果真像我听到的那样,
从来没有人从这深渊中生还,
我就不怕名誉扫地来回答你。ᵃ

那咱就去吧,你和我,
夜幕已经在天空展扩
像个病人麻醉在手术台;
咱去吧,穿过些半遭遗弃的街巷,
5 那嘈杂可退歇的地方
尽是勉强熬一宿的廉价客栈
和到处蚝壳、满地锯末的餐馆:

ᵃ 题词出自但丁《神曲·地狱篇》第 27 首,原文如下:
  "S'io credesse che mia risposta fosse
  A persona che mai tornasse al mondo,
  Questa fiamma staria senza piu scosse.
  Ma percioche giammai di questo fondo
  Non torno vivo alcun, s'i'odo il vero,
  Senza tema d'infamia ti rispondo"。
所引中文为田德望译本。艾略特引化身火焰的圭多这一段话,实为暗示普鲁弗洛克也像圭多一样,正身处地狱——现代社会的人间地狱而不能逃出,因而表露心迹也同样不怕丢人了。
* 脚注均为译者所加。

托马斯·斯特恩斯·艾略特 Thomas Stearns Eliot

那些街巷一条接一条
像居心叵测冗长乏味的呱噪
10 直把你引向一个令人窘迫的问题……
哦，别问"是啥呀？"
咱去探访一下吧。

房间里女人们来往穿梭
谈论着米开朗琪罗。

15 那黄雾用背磨蹭着玻璃窗，
那黄烟用吻磨蹭着玻璃窗，
把舌头舔进夜晚的角落，
游弋在阴沟的水洼上，
任烟囱里落下的煤烟落在背上，
20 它轻轻溜过露台，突然一跳，
见那是十月温柔的一夜，
便盘绕着房子，睡着了觉。

也确实会有时间
让那沿着街巷游弋的黄烟，
25 用背去磨蹭玻璃窗；
会有时间，会有时间
去备好一张脸去见你见的那些脸；

托马斯·斯特恩斯·艾略特 Thomas Stearns Eliot

会有时间去谋杀去创建,ª
有时间让循日劳作的双手ᵇ
30 去拈起问题放在你的餐盘;
有你的时间,有我的时间,
还有时间一百次地犹豫不定,
一百次地构想一百次地修正,
在取用吐司和茶水之前。

35 房间里女人们来往穿梭
谈论着米开朗琪罗。

也确实会有时间
去疑虑,"我敢不敢?""我敢不敢?"
有掉头走下楼梯的时间,
40 带着头顶那块脱发秃斑——
（她们会说:"他的头发稀成这样啦!"）
我的晨礼服,衣领笔挺顶到下巴,
领带奢而不华,简朴的夹子衬托着它——
（她们会说:"哦他那胳臂腿多么细呀!"）
45 我敢不敢
把宇宙搅乱?

ª 参见《圣经·传道书》第 3 章第 1-8 节:"万事都有定期,天下万务都有定时:生有时,死有时;栽种有时,拔出所种的也有时;杀戮有时,医治有时;拆毁有时,建造有时;……"
ᵇ "循日劳作":原文为古希腊赫西额德着作的标题 Works and Days。这是一部着于 8 世纪的描绘乡下生活的长篇诗作,标题曾被译作工作与时日、劳作与时日、田功农时、农作与时日等。这里根据行文所需而译。

托马斯·斯特恩斯·艾略特 Thomas Stearns Eliot

一分钟内有足够时间ᵃ
一次次决定一次次修订一分钟内又推翻。

是我早已熟悉那一切，熟悉那一切：
50 熟悉那些夜晚、早晨、下午，
我已用咖啡勺把一生量出；
熟悉在消亡式降弱中消亡的语声窃窃ᵇ
淹没它的音乐来自远处的房间。
而我该怎样妄断？

55 我也早已熟悉那些眼神，熟悉那一切——
那眼神把你用公式般套话钉起，
当我被穿在别针上，套上公式，
当我被钉在墙上扭动不迭，
我又该怎样开始
60 吐掉我一日日一种种所有的残蒂？ᶜ
我又该怎样妄断？

我也早已熟悉那些手臂，熟悉那一切——
那些手臂带着手镯、白皙而赤裸

ᵃ 典出莎士比亚喜剧《第十二夜》：开篇独白有"Even in a minute"感叹一切在爱情面前瞬间失却价值。
ᵇ "消亡式降弱"：出典同上：开篇"That strain again! It had a dying fall（又是那个调子！有一种消亡的降弱）"之句。艾略特在《一位女士的画像》中也用到此典。
ᶜ 原文"butt-ends"有双关含义。有关这一行，请参见诗人《序言》诗中"The burnt-out ends of smoky days（烟雾之日的余烬）"。

托马斯·斯特恩斯·艾略特 Thomas Stearns Eliot

（但灯光之下，淡黄绒毛满胳膊！）
65 可是衣裙上的香气
让我说话这样走题？
那些手臂横陈桌面，或裹着披肩。
我倒是该不该妄断？
我又该怎样开始？

* * * *

70 要不要说，我曾在黄昏穿过窄窄的街巷
看到孤独男人的烟斗中升起的烟缕
他们单穿衬衫，从窗口向外探着身体？……

我真该是一双粗糙的爪子
匆匆爬过那寂静的海底。

* * * *

75 而这下午，这夜晚，睡得这么安详！
修长的手指将它抚平，
它睡了……它累了……或许只是装病，
平躺在地板上，偎在你我身旁。
我该不该，吃罢茶水糕点和冰点，
80 有勇气把这一刻推到危机的顶点？

托马斯·斯特恩斯·艾略特 Thomas Stearns Eliot

可尽管我哭泣斋戒，哭泣祈祷，ᵃ
尽管看到我（略秃）的头用盘子托着来到，ᵇ
我却不是先知——也没有大事可报；ᶜ
我看到我那辉煌一刻忽闪得不妙，
85　看到那永恒的侍者捧着我的外套，窃窃发笑，ᵈ
一句话，我就是害怕。

可那值不值啊，说到底，
就算用了杯盏，吃了橘酱，喝了茶，
周围瓷器环绕，还有谈论你我的闲话，
90　那值不值啊，就算
微笑着将事情一口咬出个决断，
把宇宙揉成了一个圆球ᵉ
把球滚向那令人窘迫的问题，
去说："我是拉撒路，来自冥间，ᶠ
95　活过来对你表白，把一切告诉你"——
假如人家，塞个枕头在头边
说："我压根就不是那个用意；

ᵃ 见《圣经·撒母耳记下》第 12 节："而且他们悲哀哭号，禁食到晚上……"
ᵇ 《圣经·马可福音》第 6 章第 17-29 节和《马太福音》14:3-11 中讲到希律将施洗者约翰砍下来的头作为奖赏送给舞者。
ᶜ 《圣经·阿摩司书》第 7 章第 14 节中阿摩司说"我本不是先知，也不是先知的门徒。我只是一个牧人，也替人看护桑树"。
ᵈ 死神有时被称作"永恒的侍者"。拙译艾米莉·狄金森诗《未能停步等死神》对此意象有生动的描述。
ᵉ 源出安德鲁·马维尔诗《致他的忸怩女友》，其中有句"且把全身活力全部甜蜜/揉作一个圆球不分我你"，全诗译文见本书。
ᶠ 拉撒路：耶稣把他从墓中招回人间，见《圣经·约翰福音》第 11 章第 1-44 节。

托马斯·斯特恩斯·艾略特 Thomas Stearns Eliot

不是那回事,压根不是。"

可那值不值啊,说到底,
100 那值不值啊,就算共享过
一次次日落,一个个庭院,一条条洒水街道,
一本本小说,一只只茶杯,一条条长裙拖地——
所有这些,还有更多努力?——
我的意思根本无法说清楚!
105 但就像神灯把神经的图案投影在银幕:ᵃ
可那值不值啊,
假如人家,塞个枕头或甩掉个肩披,
然后转身面向窗口,说:
"压根不是那回事,
110 我压根就不是那个用意。"

*　*　*　*

不!我不是哈姆雷特王子,命里就不会是;ᵇ
我就是侍臣一个,我只是可以
为巡行撑个场面,弄点热闹滑稽,
给王子出个点子;确定是顺手工具,
115 恭敬而谦卑,有用很感恩,

ᵃ 神灯:可以把图像放大投影到银幕上。
ᵇ 原文"nor meant to be",典出哈姆雷特名句"To be or not to be",一语双关:既不该是王子,也不该"活着"。参见诗中"来自冥间"和"溺水死掉"之句。

托马斯·斯特恩斯·艾略特 Thomas Stearns Eliot

精明而审慎，仔细且周到；
满口高谈阔论，却略显得呆钝；ᵃ
有时候，还真近乎荒唐可笑——
有时候，还真像个大傻冒。ᵇ

120　我老啦……我老啦……
穿裤子该折起裤脚啦。ᶜ

我要不要留个后分头？吃个桃子我敢不敢？ᵈ ᵉ
我要身着白色法兰绒裤，漫步在海滩。
我听到那美人鱼在歌唱，两两相欢。ᶠ

125　我觉得她们不会对我歌唱。ᵍ

我见她们驾着海浪奔向大洋
梳理着飘向背后的浪的白发
当风把海水吹出白发和黑发。

ᵃ　"高谈阔论"原文"high sentence"出自乔叟《坎特伯雷故事集》。
ᵇ　莎士比亚多部剧中有称作"the Fool"的人物，如悲剧《李尔王》中国王的忠实奴仆兼谏言人。
ᶜ　中年危机使得主人公考虑要穿时髦服装，留前卫发式。
ᵈ　前卫得有些招眼的发式。
ᵉ　很多英文作品中用到的意象"桃子"（peach）有多重含义，既指美妙事物、美人儿，在俚语中也暗指女性阴部。
ᶠ　参阅约翰·邓恩《歌》中"Teach me to hear mermaids singing（教我去听美人鱼歌唱）。"
ᵍ　热拉尔·德·内瓦尔（Gérard de Nerval, 1808-55）有诗句"J'ai rêvé dans la grotte où nage la sirène（我梦见在洞中，塞壬在那里游泳）。"像《奥德赛》中的奥德修斯一样，普鲁弗洛克也听到塞壬的歌声，然而歌却不是唱给他听的。

托马斯·斯特恩斯·艾略特 Thomas Stearns Eliot

我们徘徊着在海洋的各个房间
130　房间被海女装了红色棕色海草
直到被人声唤醒，我们溺水死掉。

The Love Song of J. Alfred Prufrock

BY T. S. ELIOT

S'io credesse che mia risposta fosse
A persona che mai tornasse al mondo,
Questa fiamma staria senza piu scosse.
Ma percioche giammai di questo fondo
Non torno vivo alcun, s'i'odo il vero,
Senza tema d'infamia ti rispondo.

Let us go then, you and I,
When the evening is spread out against the sky
Like a patient etherized upon a table;
Let us go, through certain half-deserted streets,
5   The muttering retreats
Of restless nights in one-night cheap hotels
And sawdust restaurants with oyster-shells:
Streets that follow like a tedious argument
Of insidious intent
10 To lead you to an overwhelming question…
Oh, do not ask, "What is it?"
Let us go and make our visit.

In the room the women come and go

托马斯·斯特恩斯·艾略特 Thomas Stearns Eliot

Talking of Michelangelo.

15　The yellow fog that rubs its back upon the window-panes,
　　The yellow smoke that rubs its muzzle on the window-panes,
　　Licked its tongue into the corners of the evening,
　　Lingered upon the pools that stand in drains,
　　Let fall upon its back the soot that falls from chimneys,
20　Slipped by the terrace, made a sudden leap,
　　And seeing that it was a soft October night,
　　Curled once about the house, and fell asleep.

　　And indeed there will be time
　　For the yellow smoke that slides along the street,
25　Rubbing its back upon the window-panes;
　　There will be time, there will be time
　　To prepare a face to meet the faces that you meet;
　　There will be time to murder and create,
　　And time for all the works and days of hands
30　That lift and drop a question on your plate;
　　Time for you and time for me,
　　And time yet for a hundred indecisions,
　　And for a hundred visions and revisions,
　　Before the taking of a toast and tea.

35　In the room the women come and go
　　Talking of Michelangelo.

　　And indeed there will be time

托马斯·斯特恩斯·艾略特 Thomas Stearns Eliot

To wonder, "Do I dare?" and, "Do I dare?"
Time to turn back and descend the stair,
40　With a bald spot in the middle of my hair —
(They will say: "How his hair is growing thin!")
My morning coat, my collar mounting firmly to the chin,
My necktie rich and modest, but asserted by a simple pin —
(They will say: "But how his arms and legs are thin!")
45　Do I dare
Disturb the universe?
In a minute there is time
For decisions and revisions which a minute will reverse.

For I have known them all already, known them all:
50　Have known the evenings, mornings, afternoons,
I have measured out my life with coffee spoons;
I know the voices dying with a dying fall
Beneath the music from a farther room.
So how should I presume?

55　And I have known the eyes already, known them all—
The eyes that fix you in a formulated phrase,
And when I am formulated, sprawling on a pin,
When I am pinned and wriggling on the wall,
Then how should I begin
60　To spit out all the butt-ends of my days and ways?
And how should I presume?

And I have known the arms already, known them all—

托马斯·斯特恩斯·艾略特 Thomas Stearns Eliot

Arms that are braceleted and white and bare
(But in the lamplight, downed with light brown hair!)
65　Is it perfume from a dress
That makes me so digress?
Arms that lie along a table, or wrap about a shawl.
And should I then presume?
And how should I begin?

*　*　*　*

70　Shall I say, I have gone at dusk through narrow streets
And watched the smoke that rises from the pipes
Of lonely men in shirt-sleeves, leaning out of windows?...

I should have been a pair of ragged claws
Scuttling across the floors of silent seas.

*　*　*　*

75　And the afternoon, the evening, sleeps so peacefully!
Smoothed by long fingers,
Asleep ... tired ... or it malingers,
Stretched on the floor, here beside you and me.
Should I, after tea and cakes and ices,
80　Have the strength to force the moment to its crisis?
But though I have wept and fasted, wept and prayed,
Though I have seen my head (grown slightly bald) brought in upon a platter,

托马斯·斯特恩斯·艾略特　Thomas Stearns Eliot

I am no prophet — and here's no great matter;
I have seen the moment of my greatness flicker,
85　　And I have seen the eternal Footman hold my coat, and snicker,
And in short, I was afraid.

And would it have been worth it, after all,
After the cups, the marmalade, the tea,
Among the porcelain, among some talk of you and me,
90　　Would it have been worth while,
To have bitten off the matter with a smile,
To have squeezed the universe into a ball
To roll it towards some overwhelming question,
To say: "I am Lazarus, come from the dead,
95　　Come back to tell you all, I shall tell you all"—
If one, settling a pillow by her head
Should say: "That is not what I meant at all;
That is not it, at all."

And would it have been worth it, after all,
100　　Would it have been worth while,
After the sunsets and the dooryards and the sprinkled streets,
After the novels, after the teacups, after the skirts that trail along the floor—
And this, and so much more?—
It is impossible to say just what I mean!
105　　But as if a magic lantern threw the nerves in patterns on a screen:
Would it have been worth while
If one, settling a pillow or throwing off a shawl,

托马斯·斯特恩斯·艾略特 Thomas Stearns Eliot

  And turning toward the window, should say:
  "That is not it at all,
110 That is not what I meant, at all."

  * * * *

  No! I am not Prince Hamlet, nor was meant to be;
  Am an attendant lord, one that will do
  To swell a progress, start a scene or two,
  Advise the prince; no doubt, an easy tool,
115 Deferential, glad to be of use,
  Politic, cautious, and meticulous;
  Full of high sentence, but a bit obtuse;
  At times, indeed, almost ridiculous—
  Almost, at times, the Fool.

120 I grow old ... I grow old ...
  I shall wear the bottoms of my trousers rolled.

  Shall I part my hair behind? Do I dare to eat a peach?
  I shall wear white flannel trousers, and walk upon the beach.
  I have heard the mermaids singing, each to each.

125 I do not think that they will sing to me.

  I have seen them riding seaward on the waves
  Combing the white hair of the waves blown back
  When the wind blows the water white and black.

托马斯·斯特恩斯·艾略特 Thomas Stearns Eliot

      We have lingered in the chambers of the sea
130 By sea-girls wreathed with seaweed red and brown
      Till human voices wake us, and we drown.

切斯瓦夫·米沃什
Czesław Miłosz (1911–2004)

福赐

（散文体）

好舒心的一天。
雾一早散去，我打理花园。
有蜂鸟飞停在在金银花上。
世上没有什么物令我想占有，
也没见过什么人值得我羡慕。
遭受过的恶遇，我都忘了。
想到我还是先前的我，并不羞愧。
身上也没有病痛。
直起身来，我看到蓝色的海和船帆。

1971 于伯克利

切斯瓦夫·米沃什 Czesław Miłosz

(四言体)

舒心畅意,如此一天。
清晨雾散,理弄花园;
蜂鸟停住,金银花间。
世间万物,无欲取贪;
阅人无数,无可妒羡。
历经苦难,忘却了然;
一如故我,坦荡心安。
身无不适,拙体尚顽;
起身但见,碧海风帆。

1971 于伯克利

【译者记】尽管原诗为轻盈的散文体,我也将它译作散文体,但也做了一首四言体把玩,呈贡读者,以为消遣比较之资。

切斯瓦夫·米沃什 Czesław Miłosz

Gift

A day so happy.
Fog lifted early. I worked in the garden.
Hummingbirds were stopping over the honeysuckle flowers.
There was no thing on earth I wanted to possess.
I knew no one worth my envying him.
Whatever evil I had suffered, I forgot.
To think that once I was the same man did not embarrass me.
In my body I felt no pain.
When straightening up, I saw blue sea and sails.

Berkeley, 1971

狄兰·托马斯

Dylan Marlais Thomas (1914–1953)

而死亡也不能主宰

而死亡也不能主宰。
死者赤条条他们一定会
和风中的人西天的月合体同在；
当骨头被剔净而净骨也散尽，
繁星将萦绕他们的臂肘和脚踝；
即使发狂他们一定恢复理智，
沉殁沧海他们一定重生再来；
情侣即使消逝爱情一定长在；
而死亡也不能主宰。

而死亡也不能主宰。
展卧于波流曲折的大海
他们赴死也不会屈服摇摆；
捆绑于刑车上，挣扎在刑架上，
纵使筋骨断裂，他们也不会屈败；
信仰会随着双手一折为二，
独角兽的邪恶会把他们刺穿；
四体分裂他们也决不会崩溃；

狄兰·托马斯 Dylan Marlais Thomas

而死亡也不能主宰。

而死亡也不能主宰。
即使耳边那海鸥的啼声不再，
即使岸边那惊涛的轰鸣不再；
花开之处即使不再有花朵
昂首面对风吹雨打；
人物无论发疯还是死如铁钉，
个性的头颅也将撞穿雏菊；
驯服太阳直到太阳崩坏，
而死亡也不能主宰。

【译者记】
1、恩师巫宁坤的著名译作，尽得原诗精髓及力道，被誉为最佳译本；学生借助今天便利的研究条件，加上个人理解并调整音韵，步其后尘，致敬吾师。
2、主题出典于《新约》的《圣保罗书》："death hath no more dominion over him"，意即死亡也不能再主宰那死而复生者。

狄兰·托马斯 Dylan Marlais Thomas

And Death Shall Have no Dominion

And death shall have no dominion.
Dead men naked they shall be one
With the man in the wind and the west moon;
When their bones are picked clean and the clean bones gone,
They shall have stars at elbow and foot;
Though they go mad they shall be sane,
Though they sink through the sea they shall rise again;
Though lovers be lost love shall not;
And death shall have no dominion.

And death shall have no dominion.
Under the windings of the sea
They lying long shall not die windily;
Twisting on racks when sinews give way,
Strapped to a wheel, yet they shall not break;
Faith in their hands shall snap in two,
And the unicorn evils run them through;
Split all ends up they shan't crack;
And death shall have no dominion.

And death shall have no dominion.
No more may gulls cry at their ears
Or waves break loud on the seashores;
Where blew a flower may a flower no more
Lift its head to the blows of the rain;
Though they be mad and dead as nails,

狄兰·托马斯 Dylan Marlais Thomas

Heads of the characters hammer through daisies;
Break in the sun till the sun breaks down,
And death shall have no dominion.

狄兰·托马斯 Dylan Marlais Thomas

不要驯然遁入那个长夜

不要驯然遁入那个长夜，
老年临暮理当燃烧咆哮；
怒斥，怒斥光明竟将熄灭。

智者临终固知黑暗难却，
但因话语未作雷霆闪耀，
不会驯然遁入那个长夜。

善者尾波已尽自叹已业，
本可绿色湾中闪亮一跳，
怒斥，怒斥光明竟将熄灭。

浪者及时欢唱太阳飞跃，
辜负光阴太晚方才悟晓，
不甘驯然遁入那个长夜。

肃穆者临终凭眩灭视觉，
得见盲眼欣如流星闪耀，
怒斥，怒斥光明竟将熄灭。

而父亲您立高处空悲切，
求您挥泪骂我为我祈祷。
不要驯然遁入那个长夜。
怒斥，怒斥光明竟将熄灭。

狄兰·托马斯 Dylan Marlais Thomas

【译者记】

1、这是一首维拉内尔(villanelle)，格律甚严：五个三行诗节加一个四行诗节，五步抑扬格，韵式为 ABA ABA ABA ABA ABA ABAA，第一个诗节的一三两行作为叠句在后面的诗节末行轮流重复，并在四行诗节中共同收尾。依体作诗甚难如意，而托马斯此作堪称典范。

2、恩师巫宁坤之译品，颇得原诗精髓及力道；我谨以此译，整理音韵，步其后尘，致敬吾师。

狄兰·托马斯 Dylan Marlais Thomas

Do not go gentle into that good night

Do not go gentle into that good night,
Old age should burn and rave at close of day;
Rage, rage against the dying of the light.

Though wise men at their end know dark is right,
Because their words had forked no lightning they
Do not go gentle into that good night.

Good men, the last wave by, crying how bright
Their frail deeds might have danced in a green bay,
Rage, rage against the dying of the light.

Wild men who caught and sang the sun in flight,
And learn, too late, they grieved it on its way,
Do not go gentle into that good night.

Grave men, near death, who see with blinding sight
Blind eyes could blaze like meteors and be gay,
Rage, rage against the dying of the light.

And you, my father, there on the sad height,
Curse, bless, me now with your fierce tears, I pray.
Do not go gentle into that good night.
Rage, rage against the dying of the light.

莱昂纳德·科恩
Leonard Norman Cohen (1934–2016)

一千个吻之深

马儿在飞奔,姑娘正年轻,
成败要赌机运。
你先赢几把,便已终结——
可知连胜已尽。
轮到你去面对
你那无敌的惨败,
你把那日子当成真,
一千个吻之深。

我接客卖身,我搞定自身,[a]
我回到布吉街心。[b]
你没能抓紧,随即滑落
滑入那杰作命运。
或许我前路正漫长,
还有承诺在心:

---

[a] 原文"get fixed"含义多重:过毒瘾,弄点钱,遭修理,都有可能。
[b] 布吉街心:出自科恩另一首歌"布吉街",唱出人生挣扎和绝望,爱情的无奈和失落。

莱昂纳德·科恩 Leonard Norman Cohen

你丢弃一切只为生存，
一千个吻之深。

有时候夜长难忍受，
苦恼懦弱是我们，
咱收拾起心情抬脚走，
一千个吻之深。

性事缠身，我们转而向
大海的边际推进：
我看到那海洋已枯绝
不给我拾荒的人。
我奋力走到前甲板。
我祝福舰队残留的人——
然后任船去撞沉，
一千个吻之深。

我接客卖身，我搞定自身，
我回到布吉街心。
我猜他们不会交换礼物
那是自己的留存。
沉静是对你的想念，
完成了对你的追寻，
只是咱忘了一件事，
一千个吻之深。

莱昂纳德·科恩 Leonard Norman Cohen

有时候夜长难忍受，
苦恼懦弱是我们，
咱收拾起心情抬脚走，
一千个吻之深。

马儿在飞奔，姑娘正年轻，
成败要赌机运……

莱昂纳德·科恩 Leonard Norman Cohen

A Thousand Kisses Deep

The ponies run, the girls are young,
The odds are there to beat.
You win a while, and then it's done –
Your little winning streak.
And summoned now to deal
With your invincible defeat,
You live your life as if it's real,
A thousand kisses deep.

I'm turning tricks, I'm getting fixed,
I'm back on Boogie Street.
You lose your grip, and then you slip
Into the Masterpiece.
And maybe I had miles to drive,
And promises to keep:
You ditch it all to stay alive,
A thousand kisses deep.

And sometimes when the night is slow,
The wretched and the meek,
We gather up our hearts and go,
A thousand kisses deep.

Confined to sex, we pressed against
The limits of the sea:
I saw there were no oceans left

莱昂纳德·科恩 Leonard Norman Cohen

For scavengers like me.
I made it to the forward deck.
I blessed our remnant fleet –
And then consented to be wrecked,
A thousand kisses deep.

I'm turning tricks, I'm getting fixed,
I'm back on Boogie Street.
I guess they won't exchange the gifts
That you were meant to keep.
And quiet is the thought of you,
The file on you complete,
Except what we forgot to do,
A thousand kisses deep.

And sometimes when the night is slow,
The wretched and the meek,
We gather up our hearts and go,
A thousand kisses deep.

The ponies run, the girls are young,
The odds are there to beat …

凯伦·索利

Karen Solie (1966–)

人生就是一场狂欢

晚餐已毕，酒杯在手，隐约带着争相表露
的心思，我们追循谷歌地球那隐身老变态
穿行各自家乡的街道，却发现家乡更寒碜了，恶俗地

当代化了，剥光了儿时熟悉的当地植物，
满眼是拉毛灰泥，要么带着别样的敌意
阻止我们期待中的旧时场景

重现眼前。多可悲啊，那废弃的冰壶场——它的非法
地下室酒吧在塌陷，那颗沃尔玛的种子——
它随着人口在冒芽，那谷歌街景的永久正午。苍白

而虚高的制作价值，让调幅台的热播歌曲[a]
浮现在消退已久的社会关系网表面。我们感到
共鸣不再。不过多么可心啊那坚守不变的

斜向泊车！我们宁愿烧毁这些地方也不愿看到它们

---

[a] 调幅台的热播歌曲（hits of AM radio）：60-70 年代的流行歌曲。

凯伦·索利 Karen Solie

改变,还是就是乐意烧毁它们,这些残破之地
从那里我们带着塑入人格的创伤摇摇晃晃地走入

余生。这种地方可没法托付给四维体[a],
不过我们那个时龄已为他人所有。就像我们的老
屋。看看它被折腾成什么样子了。谁能觉得这是趣事?

要不来场音乐会吧,Youtube 上 Youtube 之前那无法想象
的日子,那时代像破产的乡村小店一样门窗都封了板
瓶瓶罐罐还在架上,我们却急急离去。多漂亮啊

那些人,穿着花哨的衣裳,唱着青春的高
音,全屏显示,有两个已不在人世。这便是
永恒?再来一个,鼓掌,再来一个;真有点身临其境了。

---

[a] 四维体(the fourfold):德国哲学家海德格尔的天地人神四维体。

凯伦·索利 Karen Solie

Life is a Carnival

Dinner finished, wine in hand, in a vaguely competitive spirit
of disclosure, we trail Google Earth's invisible pervert
through the streets of our hometowns, but find them shabbier, or
    grossly

contemporized, denuded of childhood's native flora,
stuccoed or in some other way hostile
to the historical reenactments we expect of our former

settings. What sadness in the disused curling rinks, their illegal
basement bars imploding, in the seed of a Walmart
sprouting in the demographic, in Street View's perpetual noon.
    With pale

and bloated production values, hits of AM radio rise
to the surface of a network of social relations long obsolete. We
    sense
a loss of rapport. But how sweet the persistence

of angle parking! Would we burn these places rather than see
    them
change, or just happily burn them, the sites of wreckage
from which we staggered with our formative injuries into the rest

of our lives. They cannot be consigned to the fourfold,
though the age we were belongs to someone else. Like our old

凯伦·索利 Karen Solie

house. Look what they've done to it. Who thought this would be
    fun?

A concert, then, YouTube from those inconceivable days before
YouTube, an era boarded over like a bankrupt country store,
cans still on its shelves, so hastily did we leave it. How beautiful

they are in their poncey clothes, their youthful higher
registers, fullscreen, two of them dead now. Is this
eternity? Encore, applause, encore; it's almost like being there.

凯伦·索利 Karen Solie

北方

我们该到哪儿去寻觅安慰，
既然身居北方？处于坎坷存活的
植物生命之中——它紧抠着
生命的边缘，任大气凌虐或无视
也要繁衍？带着两种心境，
既柔弱又滋蔓，它探望海外

同时本性又弯向陆内。
又何必辩解我们农业上的
强耕力作，企业上的
大胆无耻？昏昏欲睡
的愤怒中表演的深冬的
独特闹剧？有闲阶级

赞美努力工作的美德，说那
高于一切，而我们却在劳作，受制于
冰冷的规章制度和法规的黑色
字母，陷在猪臭和
崩塌的矿渣之中，刚一出生
便成中年，全心全意地

诽谤这个地方，莫名其妙地
仇外。与其说超然其上

凯伦·索利 Karen Solie

还不如就迁移南下。同情之心
跟维生之举难道就
不可分割吗?自我还能是啥
除了跟寒冷搏斗?

凯伦 • 索利 Karen Solie

The North

Where should we find consolation,
dwelling in the north? Amid the stunted
desperate plant life clinging
to its edges, thriving on atmospheric
vengeance or neglect? Of two moods,
fragile and invasive, it gazes out to sea

as its character bends inland.
And why defend our poignant attempts
at agriculture, the gall
of our entrepreneurs? The defining
mid-winter pageants performed
in a somnolent rage? The leisure class

commends the virtues of hard work
above all else, and we labour under
frost-cramped statutes, the black
letters of legislation, in hog-reek
and land-driven slag, middle-aged
from birth and, given our devotion

to slandering this place, illogically
xenophobic. We could as soon move
south as rise above it. Are sympathies
inseparable from what one does
to stay alive? What is a self
but that which fights the cold?

凯伦·索利 Karen Solie

改建

仓促一览的第一印象。是万能
溶剂,还有床底的魔障。一股既
抱歉又敌意的气息,一些被遗弃的
用具来自甩卖场,窗帘材料是化纤的

也是虔诚的,其份量和能量都足以
吸收愧罪感。这兴旺生态系统的栖居者
从织料的毛边和破败踢脚板的边缘
探望一阵,就壮起胆来。一只门把手

脱落在我手里,像个荒唐的假肢。
这类的房间到处黏着我都已经
二十年了。好像我嫁入了表亲众多
的糟糕人家。而我是那唯一

爱他们的人。我就是这种感觉。
就算一个家庭牛排馆把呛人的废气
排放进我的门槛,就算带着重现的谜团,
那蛾子是如何进来的谜团——

一到早晨它们就用自身的钩子把自己
无处不在地挂起,像一件件小外套——
我照样安然处于这不操闲心的奢侈之中。

凯伦·索利 Karen Solie

这是一种技能,就像系鞋带。其他一切

都失去了,技能还会在。燃气爆炸
摧毁了美景山汽车旅馆东翼,使之仅仅
略微不适合居住的责任——尽管没有登记

在册——依然是,一个秘密
藏在重建的房中。借烧渣砖和柏油屋顶
之形再次立起,一副天真,名称照旧,仿佛
本可积累的还有待来日。不要

再次派我去那个地方。那最后一晚
在鲑鱼湾,也可能是温赖特,韶那氖,或
者苏城[a],不管是哪儿,那最后内置的又外垮,
或外展的又内垮了,我想起了你呢。

---

[a] 鲑鱼湾、温赖特、韶那氖、苏城(Salmon Arm, Wainwright, Shaunavon, The Sault)都是加拿大的小城镇,分属卑诗省,埃尔伯塔省,萨斯喀彻温省和安大略省。

凯伦·索利 Karen Solie

Conversion

First impression of a hasty once-over. Of universal
solvent and under-the-bed. An atmosphere both
apologetic and hostile, orphaned
amenities procured at clearance, curtains synthetic

and religious in their weight and ability
to absorb guilt. A thriving ecosystem's residents
stared from fringes of the textiles, the debased
baseboards, and would grow bold. A doorknob

came off in my hand like a joke prosthetic.
Rooms like this have followed me around
for 20 years. It's as though I married into a bad
family of many cousins. I was the only one

who loved them. That's what I thought.
Even as a family steakhouse vented its cruel exhaust
across my threshold, even in the resurrected mystery
of how the moths get in –

by morning they'd hung themselves everywhere
like little coats by their own hooks –
I was at peace in the luxury of all that lack of care.
It was a skill, like tying knots. When all else

had gone, it would be there. Blame

凯伦·索利 Karen Solie

for the propane explosion that destroyed the east wing
of the Monte Vista Motel, rendering it only slightly
less habitable, though not registered

in the paperwork, remains, a secret
crouched in the rebuild. In cinder block and flat tarred
roof it rose again, innocent, under the same name, as if
what could accrue had yet to do so. Don't

send me back out there again. That final night
in Salmon Arm, maybe Wainwright, Shaunavon or
The Sault, wherever it was the last built-in fell out,
or the fold-out fell in, I thought of you then.

www.ingramcontent.com/pod-product-compliance
Lightning Source LLC
Chambersburg PA
CBHW060608080526
44585CB00013B/736